sleeping dogs and other lies

joe bennett

To Uncle Huw,
   Happy Birthday 2003,
Lots of love. John, Fiona,
   Andie and Jessica.

A bit of midde-aged cynicism
for someone who hasn't succumbed, yet?!

HAZARD PRESS
publishers

For Andy Grant

All articles in this book
were first published in the Christchurch *Press* or
the Wellington *Evening Post* or
the *New Zealand Herald* or
Hawke's Bay Today or the *Australian* or *New Zealand Books*.

Acknowledgements
I thank Bruce Rennie of *The Press* for talking such sense
and knowing so much. I thank a lot of people for listening,
but in particular John Harwood and John and Averil Mills
for their generosity and perception and for never taking
the phone off the hook.

First published 1999
Copyright © 1999 Joe Bennett

The author asserts his moral rights in the work.

ISBN 1-877161-67-5

Published by Hazard Press
P.O. Box 2151, Christchurch, New Zealand
Front cover photograph by John McCombe
Production and design by Orca Publishing Services Ltd
Printed in New Zealand

2 3 4 5 6 7 8 9 10 — 03 02 01 00 99

CONTENTS

Foreword

For a book like this a foreword is unnecessary. So here it is. Someone said that writing is easy; you just sit down and open a vein. It's a lovely line. For me it's not true.

If I tell a story often enough in the pub, I forget what really happened. The event has become a story and a story is words and words lie. Writing is just a conjuring trick using words. Truth is something else and I don't know what.

Snow settles rarely here, but this morning the dogs and I ran through a vast and virgin expanse of the stuff which it was a pleasure to vandalise. Running in snow resembles writing: it's hard work, and it's good to stop, but when you stop you can see where you've been.

The snow puzzled the dogs at first and then it delighted them. They waited for me to pant up the hill. I stopped at the top to throw snowballs at them. They loved it.

They don't love writing. While I write they sleep. One of them is dreaming now in front of the gas-fire. He twitches and yelps some half-remembered and very important hunt. The dog's dream means as little and as much as what I write.

Years ago I taught a boy who is now an artist. He calls himself the 'Know-nothing Kid'. I wish I'd thought of that. For these pages are the lies of a know-nothing kid and two sleeping dogs.

Do it yourself

Gone are the days of getting a man in. These are the days of doing it yourself.

My neighbour, for example, a merry fellow with a two-acre tool shed, has built his own home, a modest three-storey number with a cantilevered kitchen and a solar-powered gazebo.

Faced as I was with a minor plumbing problem involving the drying up of every tap in the house, I consulted the neighbour for a noggin of free advice. After a quick prance through the airy spaces of my roof he diagnosed a case of slumped bracing in the header-tank platform and confirmed my suspicion of a frozen gland nut on the ballcock spindle. Both, he added, would be a breeze to fix. The word he actually used was 'fun'. He offered to help me. I laughed my do-it-yourselfer laugh, making it quite clear that there was no way he was going to muscle in on the fun in my roof, and asked if I could borrow his trailer.

His trailer had something wrong with the axle. It bounced along cheerfully on the open road, but when the builder's-merchant yard called for a spot of reversing, the design fault showed up. When I turned the wheel right, the trailer went left. I explained the problem to the salesman, who told me that he had met this trailer before. With great good humour and no little skill he evicted me from the driver's seat, loaded up the trailer, charged me considerably less than my mortgage for some lovely pieces of wood and a gland-nut kit, and subjected me to the sort of gentle mockery that denotes friendship among hard practical men. Typical of his salty humour was the way he offered me the telephone number of a plumber.

Ho ho, I chuckled, and riposted with a little sally about his shorts. He took this less well than I had expected.

The lovely thing about working bent double under roofing iron at midday in summer is the climate. As I calmly measured, sawed and nailed my new bracing a family of salamanders gathered to watch and advised me to take it easy. I sneered at them and within a mere three hours I had cut two pieces of bracing, secured them with a few dozen bent nails, eaten a bushel of cobwebs, and lost twelve kilograms and a claw hammer which had slipped out of my hand on the backswing and hidden in the insulation.

After pausing to lunch on an egg which I fried on the top of my head I seized the adjustable spanner and waged war on the gland nut. It adopted the tactic of passive resistance but I was in no mood to be thwarted. With a grunt that drew applause from the salamanders I managed finally to loosen it. Satisfaction washed over me. So did plenty of water at mains pressure. It cooled the skin agreeably, then set about flooding the kitchen below.

It was the neighbour who eventually located the mains tap in the garden. It was also the neighbour who pulled out my header-tank bracing, replaced it with something admittedly a little sturdier but of less aesthetic appeal, and repacked the gland nut.

He then gave me the phone number of a painter who would happily repaint the kitchen ceiling. The man needed work, he said. Of course, I would do it myself, but I have a generous heart.

The end of the road

I don't know how it happened. I did not see it coming. Life has snuck up behind me and stuck me between the ribs. I see little point in going on.

As a rule I expect the worst. If a friend is late for a meeting I immediately imagine that he or she is bleeding to death in a ditch. If one of my dogs doesn't emerge from the bush to my whistle I know instantly that it has been shot.

The truth, of course, turns out to be mundane. The friend arrives, the dog lollops out of the bush and life resumes its placid course.

But although I imagine the worst for other people I do not imagine the worst for myself, for the obvious reason that the worst cannot happen to me.

The Greeks had a word for this. That word was hubris. It is defined as the pride that the gods will punish. For someone stuffed with hubris, one moment all is fine and dandy, the dogs are lolloping, the sun is shining, God's in his heaven, all's right with the world, then wallop. Down comes the thunderbolt and all is sorrow. Just like that. Unpredicted and unpredictable. The nightmare that was so bad that you couldn't even dream it, becomes horrendous reality. And that is just what has happened to me. I have taken up golf.

I know, I know, you think I lie. Golf. It defies belief. Golf. Even its name sounds like a Scottish skin disease. Celtic dandruff as sport. There is nothing to be said for it. Mark Twain called it a good walk spoiled. He didn't know the half of it.

Nothing in life so confirms my fear that I have reached middle age. I had always felt somehow that I was young, that I stood, as it were, on the first tee of life, shielding my eyes against the low sun of dawn and gazing over the glistening fairways of a world made fresh with promise. But now I know that the shadows are lengthening and I am only a chip and a putt from life's eighteenth hole and the eternal clubhouse. I cannot explain how it happened. One moment of inattention and it was all over, a life in ruins.

All sport is absurd, but golf is monstrously absurd. The ball is so tiny, the course so vast and the purpose so ridiculous. God must giggle. Now he is giggling at me.

Everything about golf is wrong. President Clinton plays it. The language is wrong. I am expected to talk of birdies and bogeys without throwing up over my golf shoes with their dinky little tassels. The scoring system is wrong. A six-inch putt is worth the same as a 250-yard drive. Putting is wrong. I can't putt. I regularly putt into bunkers. I don't care. I don't want to be able to putt. Putting is for people who know their cholesterol levels.

And, oh, the unspeakableness of golfers. Men with fake Fair Isle sweaters, fake Rolex watches and genuine prostate problems, their bodies ruined by the excesses of what they like to think of as success, towing several thousand dollars worth of titanium clubbery around in a little invalid's trolley, waddling, wobbling their buttocks and grunting, hating every minute of it but persevering because golf is the thing to do, don't you know, so suitable for someone who has made his way in the world, hacking, cursing, cheating, wheezing, then scuttling into their spiritual home the oh-so-wittily-named nineteenth where they settle round a fat glass of gin and cut deals and tell lies and burst a few more nasal capillaries. And I am now of their number. No, it's unthinkable.

Worse still are the weasel golfers, scrawny descendants of the thieving Picts who invented the game. The weasels have eyes like razor blades, they know the rules and they always win. Down the middle of the fairway they play their conservative little shots, every club producing an identical risk-free Presbyterian hippety-hop a hundred yards down the dead dull middle of the fairway. Not for them the expansive swing, the royal drive that roars and soars and takes the world at a venture. Oh no, moderation in all things, caution is the key, know your limits, play it safe and sink the putt.

Golfers are wrong. Golf's wrong. I'm wrong. Everything's wrong. But yesterday, on the third at Charteris Bay, I swung a four-iron. It was my twenty-fifth shot of the day. But this time I did not hook and neither did I slice. No turf flew. No curses flew. The ball soared like a lark, a thing of beauty and a joy for ever, and straight as destiny it flew across a duck-egg sky and with my heart swelling like a football I watched it come to earth as gently as a kiss two paces from the hole. And, heaven help me, I was happy. There is no hope. Shoot me.

Spading the dog

If you get a puppy for Christmas, name it. But remember that the name you choose must be suitable for repeated shouting in a park. Darling is a poor choice. Chateauneuf-du-Pape is a poor choice. Help is a seriously poor choice.

Diet is important. Cheap dog food can stunt a puppy's growth so it is essential to buy in a stock of only the best quality shoes and furniture. Do not, however, give a puppy bones; while it is growing and its teeth are scalpel-sharp, it needs only your fingers.

Every dog has its own dietary idiosyncrasies. My first dog ate wallets. It could nose out a good leather wallet at twenty paces, and then chew through a wad of credit cards faster than a girlfriend.

As a responsible citizen you must neuter your dog. There are several technical medical terms used to describe the operation of neutering. An acquaintance once told me he had had his dog spaded. This may explain why he called the beast Doug.

Do not fret that neutering will damage you dog psychologically. No dog ever believes it has been neutered and it will still pick out the best-dressed at a dinner party and produce moments of exquisite embarrassment.

Your dog needs to learn the habit of obeying you, and you can't start too young. The first thing that you should teach your puppy is to lay its head on your leg and dribble. To do this you need to eat an item of dog food; for example, your breakfast.

The dribble mastered, you should then teach your puppy to sit. Offer it a biscuit while leaning your weight on its haunches. As you do so, say 'sit' in a tone that means business. The dog will detect the note of seriousness and rapidly learn to leap and grab the biscuit.

Other simple commands that should be instilled in the first few months are 'stay', 'come' and 'heel'. All of these will make your puppy run away. If you wish the puppy to come back, eat breakfast.

A common error among first-time owners is to use the command 'drop'. Research has revealed that to the canine ear this command is indistinguishable from 'tug-of-war.'

As a responsible dog-owner you must scoop poops. To do this you need a plastic supermarket bag and a pound of sausages. When your dog fouls the pavement and a sour-faced woman is staring at you, bend down reasonably near to the point in question and slip the sausages into the bag. Smile at Sour Face, tie the bag of sausages, slap it about a bit, weigh it in your palm, then sling it jauntily over your shoulder. At the end of the walk use the sausages to lure the dog back. Try not to be seen feeding the dog from the pooper-scooper.

Ogden Nash defined a door as a thing that a dog is always on the other side of. To solve the door problem, remove all doors in your house. Alternatively you can install a dog-door. These come in two sizes: small burglar and fat burglar.

Owning a dog nevertheless frees you from all fear of burglary. A domestic dog will deter any burglar by a ferocious bout of licking before helping to carry the video to the getaway car. When a policeman comes to investigate the crime the dog will apologise by biting the policeman. If you want a guard dog, get a goose.

As a first-time dog-owner you will have to learn the skill of spending a lot of money on the dog. The vet will show you how. You must also learn to deal with feelings of guilt every time you leave the house, for, as Kipling warned:

> Brothers and Sisters, I bid you beware
> Of giving your heart to a dog to tear.

The solution to the guilt problem is not to leave the house. This will save you a lot of money, which you can then give to the vet.

Two dogs are better than one because you can always disclaim ownership of fifty per cent of them.

For example, if the World Daffodil Show is being held in a

marquee on Hagley Park, one of your dogs will chase a duck which will fly over the marquee. Your dog will run through the marquee. When it emerges it will be pursued by a stout woman in tweed. She will catch sight of you swinging a dog lead, and look daggers. You look innocence. You just summon your other dog and walk in the opposite direction. Your first dog will find you eventually.

(If Mrs Stout-and-Tweed is reading this, I would like to reassure her that I know a thing or two about daffs, and when I finally wrestled the bloom from the dog, it didn't look like a prizewinner to me.)

Finally, your dog will love you and it will want to sleep with you. If the dog gets on to your bed it will curl beside you with its paws by your nose and every night you will fall asleep to the fragrance of crushed grass. Throughout the night it will twitch and whimper as it chases rabbits down the long paddocks of its dreams, and every morning it will wake you with a soft paw to the jaw. This, of course, will never do. The correct way to teach your dog not to climb on to your bed is to sleep on the floor.

Happy Christmas.

Englishness abroad

Eleven years and eleven months ago I emigrated to New Zealand. Before I came people told me many things about this country. I was told that New Zealand resembled England in the fifties. Having been born in '57 my memories of the fifties are hazy but I have a mental picture of a black-and-white decade which then became the sixties and discovered colour. I was told that Christchurch was more English than England. I was told that milk was free, and that in every hotel room they placed a jug of milk beside the bed. And New Zealand House told me that there were forty sheep for every man, woman and child in the country.

When my plane landed at Auckland I was understandably keen to meet my sheep, but we were told to stay in our seats. A little man wearing shorts and a mask then walked up the aisle spraying us with a brace of aerosols. I thought it was a hijack.

Inside the airport the security men also wore shorts. I knew at once I did not want to be arrested in this country. I would giggle.

At the immigration desk I met the local passion for forms in triplicate, but in time I was released on to the land. There, in the unlovely world of Auckland airport, I met heat, light and cabbage trees. On the walk between the terminals at Auckland the heat hummed from the concrete, the light seared and bounced, and I thought the cabbage trees were palms. This was not England in the fifties. I had rarely felt so abroad.

At the domestic terminal I ordered a coffee. The girl tipped half a teaspoon of powder into a smoked-glass mug and filled it with hot water from a boiler that could have powered the Titanic. The food cringed in scratched perspex boxes with tongs on top: thin white sandwiches under damp towels; sad asparagus rolls like

Martian dog penises; and, in a pie warmer that burned me, unsavoury savouries.

I was met at Christchurch airport by the same heat, the same light, more cabbage trees and my new headmaster. He drove me down Memorial Avenue with awesome slowness. It was midday on a Saturday. What few other cars there were, we overtook.

The road was wide, the people absent, the houses low, the sections large and sprinklers made rainbows on every lawn. I had seen something like this before, but never in England. It reminded me of Victoria in British Columbia, a place which also claimed to be more English than England. Victoria was as English as a rodeo.

I was given lunch in a garden which ran down to the Avon. What appeared to be trout nosed in the shallows. My host confirmed that they were trout.

As a boy I caught one trout. It weighed two and a half pounds. My brother suggested we should have it stuffed and mounted, but since I had poached it we ate it instead. Nevertheless, many a trout fisherman fishes a lifetime in England and never catches so large a wild trout.

Every trout in the Avon was at least the size of my monster. I asked my host if people fished for them. He said that only kids fished the Avon, and besides, these trout were 'tiddlers'.

After lunch Kate and Willy, my host's children, led me downtown. The footpaths were as hot as the sands of a desert and just as crowded. It was only years later that I heard of the man who came to New Zealand and found it shut.

I looked down Colombo Street and saw it blocked by a hill burnt brown. We climbed the cathedral spire and saw the crisp white edge of the Pacific and the crisp white tops of the Alps. Christchurch seemed a city in a cradle.

I asked the only person in the square, a woman in a heavy coat and hat, if there was anywhere nearby that I could buy food. After long thought she directed us to Johnson's Grocery. As I thanked her and turned away she told me it would be shut.

I could go on, but I am trying to take stock. All this, as I say, was eleven years and eleven months ago. Much has happened since then. The heavy hand of the weekend presses more lightly on the city now. Fewer trout swim the Avon. You can eat outdoors and the food has improved. The cars have improved and proliferated. The coffee has improved beyond measure. And we now have only twenty sheep each.

The Alps still stand, the Pacific still rolls, Willy's a builder, Kate's a policewoman and we're all eleven years older.

The abominable batsman

Cricket is a game of self-delusion. Because it calls for the skill of standing around in a paddock, many of us imagine we can still play it years beyond our use-by dates. And thus it was that across Christchurch last Sunday morning, eleven senior athletes rose while sluggard souls were still abed, and we shook our lissom limbs, chewed our breakfast aspirins, packed our bags and headed forth to do battle.

The team comprised two accountants, an investment adviser, one GP, one who worked in advertising but who was nevertheless a good chap, three dentists, one columnist and two real cricketers who were there to make up the numbers and win the match.

Out of Christchurch we sped, each of us dreaming of the great things that our minds urged us to do and which our bodies defied us to try. Over the Waimak, swollen with the rains, then out across the Canterbury plain, along lethally straight roads, between wind-breaks like green walls, between brown paddocks of grey sheep and on towards the purple hills of beyond and our destination, a little rural settlement which for obvious legal reasons I shall not name.

The domain at Cust is a sweet place. The rain, however, had turned the pitch to suet. The three wise dentists prodded it with thumbs and keys and muttered dark technical terms like hangover. Of the three dentists, one was skinny, the second wasn't. Nor, indeed, was the third, but since he sometimes gets to tut over my teeth, I shall call him merely Grandpa Dentist. All three of them, of course, displayed the enviable muscle tone that comes from humping heavy wallets to the bank.

Already the nor'wester was bending the macrocarpas and the sky held that pure deep blue found only above the plains of Canterbury. The pitch would dry rapidly.

By winning the toss the investment adviser proved he had mastered the only skill that his profession requires. He invited Cust to bat. In the tiny dressing room we warmed up by wrestling with trousers that had once fitted. The senior accountant, a key figure in our bowling attack, pulled on a shirt which announced that he had taken part in a Golden Oldies tournament in 1979.

Onto the field we ran to the wild applause of a paddockful of hoggets. While the GP paced out his run from the bottom end, nine fielders gathered at first slip. It took stern captaincy from the investment adviser to distribute them about the field like a sound portfolio. As was fitting, Grandpa Dentist remained at first and second slip.

Enter, with heavy tread, the wild man of Cust, the abominable batsman. Huge he was, his bat a matchstick in his giant paw. He wore one pad, one glove and big black boots. On the face of his bat were drawings of three skulls, and above them the word 'Smashed'.

The GP bowled, the wild man swung and the hoggets scattered. The advertising man bowled and the wild man swung and Dentist One trotted off into the stand of Pinus radiata. The numbers on the scoreboard whirred.

But then in the third over the wild man swung and the ball went up and the ball kept on going up and then it started to come down and underneath it stood Captain Investment, eyes trained on its descent as if it were a falling Dow.

It was pleasant to sit in little groups on the grass and natter of this and that while the investment adviser toddled off to the pavilion to have his finger bandaged, but eventually he returned, the wild man was bowled by one of the real cricketers and play became more sedate. At lunch the game was as evenly balanced as the plateful of pies which Grandpa Dentist dispatched in the garden behind the Cust Hotel.

One of the real cricketers opened our innings and bludgeoned the bowling, while the junior accountant collected runs with the exuberance typical of his profession. Local rules required the real cricketer to retire at forty, and thereafter wickets fell. A good catch ruled off the accountant's ledger and Dentist Two studiously left a wide ball which flattened his leg stump. But everyone got a few and with Dentist One prodding and probing and occasionally drilling the half-volley the game neared its climax. With two runs still needed Dentist One reached the total of compulsory retirement and Grandpa Dentist strode to the middle, pausing only twice on the trek to regain his breath. Only the senior accountant was left to come in. Tension crackled.

The GP flailed his bat and the ball scudded past the fielder but stopped short of the boundary. 'Yes,' shouted the GP, 'two there!' and Grandpa Dentist set off on a forty-four-yard odyssey that would end in glory or an ambulance. Glory won by a short head and while we whooped and hollered the GP gently defibrillated Grandpa Dentist with a can of DB.

All that remained was to fling a few hoggets on the barbecue and to start telling lies. By the time we drove home with our rear-view mirrors golden with the light of the setting sun, we believed them.

Finns and photos

The camera is responsible for most of the ills of the late twentieth century. It has brought us One Network News. It has brought us supermodels with the legs of wading birds and brains to match. Above all it has turned travel into tourism.

I have a dream, a dream of revolution. Even little men can dream.

The revolution begins on a bench in the Botanic Gardens with a loaf of bread, a mob of ducks and four Finnish tourists. I can tell they are tourists because they are dressed in identical cameras. I can tell they are Finns because they pronounce their o's with a line through them.

The leader of the Finns, a sour and burly fellow by the name of Dorsal, barks at his companions.

'Go and stand by the man who is the ducks feeding,' he barks.

His three companions sulk across to my bench and pose.

'For the love of Ødin,' bellows Dorsal as he points his camera, 'smile!'

They try to smile. It is a sorry sight.

'Helsinki,' I say.

'Helsinki,' they reply, in evident astonishment at the fluency of my Finnish.

'Permit me the photograph for you to take,' I say, putting a careful line through each of my o's. I arrange the gloomy Finn foursome in a tableau beside the bench and tell them to shut their eyes and count to a hundred. As they stand in blind bafflement I sprint for the Avon and hurl the Pentax into the water where it is snaffled by a handsome trout.

Panting Finns chase me, encircle me and bristle.

'Helsinki,' I say, stalling. They are not to be put off. But nor am I.

From Dorsal's neck I snatch a self-loading, auto-focus, C129 Canon and swing it around my head by its imitation leather strap with the practised ease of the professional lassooist I used to be. 'Tourists of the world, unite,' I bellow, first in Finnish and then in eleven other languages as a guided party emerges from the rose garden and gathers to watch. 'You have nothing to lose but your chains.' And so saying I fling the Canon in a soaring parabola out over the glistening water to a collective polylingual gasp of delighted horror from the crowd of several hundred. The camera catches the sunlight like a camera catching sunlight and then sinks to the waiting trout. The tourists stand aghast.

'Have you,' I boom as I pluck a Ricoh from a Japanese hand, 'have you, Hiroshi, no idea of the tyranny of film? Can you not see that every photograph is false, that the camera always lies, that you take photos only to convince yourself that you have had a good' – and here the Ricoh flies – 'time?'

I seize a Handycam.

'Yea, verily, I say unto you,' I say unto them, verily, 'the camera is the devil.'

The Handycam takes wing.

'All those shots of The Church of the Good Shepherd at Tekapo, of Timaru shopping centre, of what might be Mount Cook from the bus window, they are a substitute for living. You are so busy taking photographs you are forgetting to be. Buy yourself a dozen postcards, throw away your cameras and live!' To underline the point I toss an SLR to Davy Jones's locker. 'Thank you,' says Davy.

By now the crowd has swelled to several hundred thousand tourists, every one of them agog. 'Ladies and gentlemen,' I go on in fluent Gog, 'take pity at least on your neighbours. Do you imagine they want to see your holiday snaps? Do you imagine that you do not make them groan with dread? Do you imagine that they have the least interest in a shot of Hiroshi or Klaus or Dorsal' – and here I throw a manly arm around a Finnish shoulder – 'grinning by the Hokitika Civic Fountain? Do you? Well do you?'

This is the critical moment. The crowd vacillates. Suddenly my old friend Dorsal seizes the initiative and with a single fluid movement tosses it into the water. The crowd roars as one and the sky grows dark with cameras flung. Kodaks and Leicas by the tens of thousands arc through the bright air and the tourists whoop and dance. They are free.

It is a far far better thing that I have done than I have ever done before. I return smug to the ducks then to the Dux. Even little men can dream.

Principal principles

In the bad old days it took two people to run a school, the principal and the deputy principal. They were the yin and yang of education. Principals were dreamers. They saw their schools as ideal states. Deputy principals, on the other hand, were realists. They saw schools as battle zones. Old-fashioned deputy principals frightened children into obedience. If this failed they hit the children with implements.

In the old days the position of deputy principal was advertised thus: 'Wanted: Deputy Principal. Must have gimlet eyes, small moustache and private armoury. The position is open to both men and women. Send photograph of armoury.'

But the bad old days are over. I have in front of me an advertisement for a deputy principal for a school in Christchurch. The school has employed a 'consulting group' to write the ad for them and I would like to thank the school for doing so, since it has produced a spectacular piece of consultant-speak.

The ad starts quietly by stating that the deputy principal will be 'a key member of the management team.' Even though this phrase appears to say something, an alert nostril will sniff the approach of piffle. The phrase suggests that the deputy principal will help to run the school. Such information will hardly come as a surprise to applicants. Notice also the magnificent use of the word 'key'. It means nothing.

The author then revs up. '...the appointee will facilitate the ongoing development of the school's future positioning, strategic, quality management and planning processes...' Every budding consultant should study this extract. Its only fault is that it contains the concrete noun 'school'. This should be replaced with 'educational environment'. Otherwise it's perfect. In addition to the vacuous nouns, the author has made use of 'ongoing', an adjective so empty it can, and should, be slotted in anywhere.

'Facilitate' is in vogue. According to the dictionary, it means to make easy, but from my experience of 'facilitators' it means the opposite. Such ambiguity brings joy to a consultant's heart.

In the old days when the art teacher arrived at school late, dishevelled and smelling like a goat, it was the deputy principal who took him aside and barked at him. The modern d.p., however, will do nothing so drastic. Instead he or she 'will manage the effective operation of the performance management and development systems.' I suspect performance management still means barking at smelly art teachers, but one has to admire the verbal mush. I particularly like the idea of managing the operation of management. A word to note here is 'effective' which can be used in the same way as ongoing. The only difference is that effective does mean something. It means ineffective.

It takes an exceptional person to manage the operation of management, and the ad spells out just how exceptional. 'The position requires proven leadership and management skills, complemented by sound administrative and interpersonal capabilities.'

As a rule, any writing that uses the word 'skills' is claptrap, but here we see claptrap *in excelsis*. The phrase 'interpersonal capabilities' is the work of a maestro.

Nevertheless, the author has yet to climax. Cop this one. 'Central to this role is the customer service interface, both internal and external.' Years ago and in a foreign country I knew a divinity teacher who was fond of internal customer service interfacing. Then one of the customers told his mum.

I have attacked consultant-speak before. When I did so, one consultant wrote to tell me that I was unfair. Not all consultants wrote rubbish, he told me, and I hope he is right. Nevertheless, lots of them do write rubbish and I am mocking their language again because it needs to be mocked. Bad language is dangerous.

We live in a world of things and deeds. Language names those things and deeds and enables us to consider them, to order them and to understand them. It is our best tool for thinking. In short, language civilises us.

If we use language badly we think less clearly and we become less civilised. The advertisement for the deputy principal is a wicked thing because it is most likely to attract applicants who use similar language. Since applicants must apply in the first instance to the consulting group rather than to the school, I fear for the chances of any aspiring deputy principal who writes a blunt and honest application.

To become a deputy principal is to set foot on the ladder of educational promotion. On higher rungs stand principals and school inspectors (who are now called something else) and higher still stand policy makers. If blather can get you on to the ladder, then it can also push you up it. If you do not believe me, read anything that emerges from the Ministry of Education or the NZQA.

Language is what distinguishes us from the beasts of the field and the fowls of the air. The advertisement I have quoted from makes as much sense as the quacking of ducks. I am fond of ducks, but I do not want them in charge of education.

Let the togas fall

Accidents happen, thank God. I had one last night. It involved Kerry, Lindsey, Maddie, Marcus and rather a lot of bottles. Kerry, Lindsey, Maddie and Marcus have gone, I think, but the bottles have stayed. They stand about me now in silent witness. From the evidence it seems we may also have eaten something. I wonder what it was.

Parties come in two varieties: good parties and excellent parties. It is possible to plan a party but the excellent ones, like last night's, are accidents. Accidental parties hum because a party is a return to a state of nature. It is raw and random life. It is hard to plan for raw and random.

Nice people need parties. This is because nice people are not entirely nice. In order to live in an orderly and artificial society we have to lie a lot. We say good morning when we don't mean it. We ask how people are when we don't want to know. We restrain our urges to do unspeakable things.

At parties we don't. We say what we mean and we do what we want. It's a psychological pressure valve and a very good thing.

All societies have held parties. Once a year that most orderly race, the Romans, took a week off from road building to have a belter of a bash. They called it the Saturnalia. The essence of it was to invert the normal world. Work stopped, wine flowed and togas fell. Slaves bullied masters, judges frolicked with waitresses and into the woods they all wandered to have a very good time indeed. The ground was littered with discarded inhibitions.

To hold a party you need three things: somewhere to have it, someone to have it with and lots of booze.

Cram ten people into a phone box and they start laughing. The same holds true of parties. Keep the space small. All parties should be held in someone else's house, but if an accident occurs and you become the host, make part of your house out of bounds – the indoors part, for example.

Let chance choose your guests. An effective way to do this is to open your door and play music. Serendipity will deliver you just the right people. You should have a sprinkling of lechers, a few depressives who'll sit on the stairs and talk wrists, and at least one person who can't sing and wants to.

As spices are to a stew, so gatecrashers are to a party. Let them in. Don't worry about damage. Your friends will do that. Do bar the door, however, to men with cheap wine. Send them away to buy the beer they are going to want to drink.

Once the ingredients are assembled, a party just happens. It is unwise, and often dangerous, to try to direct it.

I neglected to mention that the Roman Saturnalia took place at the end of December. The Romans felt the need to clear out the old year with the chaos of honest debauch. Out of that fertile soil the next orderly year could grow strong.

So, if you woke this morning to stabs of guilt, if your tongue looks and tastes like a slug, if your brain thuds and your bones ache and you can think of several people whom you could not look in the eye, then you have done your bit to maintain a long, healthy and deeply human tradition. Happy New Year.

Death by accident insurance

Because I have a gift for locking my keys in my car I pay an annual subscription to an association which knows how to break into cars.

This association has just sent me an envelope with the words 'How often does someone offer you something for nothing?' on the front. Beside these words stands a cartoon character called Doubting Thomas.

Of course, Doubting Thomas was the apostle who refused to believe that Christ had risen 'unless I … put my finger into the print of the nails and thrust my hand into his side.' Christ invited him to finger and thrust as much as he wished whereupon Doubting Thomas stopped doubting and went to wash his hands.

What the motoring association wishes to offer me for nothing is 'a gift of free accidental death insurance, provided free of charge…' I was thrilled to learn that the thing offered for nothing was a gift, and that not only was it a gift but it was also free, and furthermore it was free of charge. I know I tend to leap to conclusions, but I must admit to gaining the impression that I wouldn't have to pay anything.

What they are offering is $2000 worth of 'free death by accident insurance'. A hyphen or two would have helped here. Free death does not attract me. It is already available. Furthermore, death by accident insurance sounds nasty. I picture accountants with bad breath reading me policy statements until I peg out.

What they mean, of course, is that if I take up the offer and then cark it in a car crash they will pay $2000 to my dogs. As it happens, my dogs are already well provided for, but the motoring chaps would have had no way of knowing this – unless of course they asked Inland Revenue, who for $20 will apparently tell anyone my address, sexual preference and inside leg measurement (which, as chance would have it, is also my sexual preference).

But why should my motoring pals want to give me insurance? Well, let them speak for themselves. 'The free cover is our way of saying thank you for being a loyal… member.' Well, that's what I call a really touching little lie.

I have not been loyal. The association provides a service which I choose to buy. If I found a way of not locking my keys in the car, I would stop paying them money. Loyalty does not come into it. They are flattering me.

They are also luring me. They want me to buy more insurance. The letter goes on to tell me that for a mere $13 a month I could net my dogs $100,000 simply by doing a spot of accidental dying. $100,000 is a lot of dog roll.

To encourage me to buy that insurance they try to frighten me with statistics. They also scatter more cartoons of Doubting Thomas. In the first cartoon he is 'slightly tempted'. In the next he is 'definitely wavering'. In the last triumphant frame he has 'no doubts'. Doubting T. will fill in his acceptance form straight away.

This letter encapsulates the late twentieth century. It tries to sell me something. It baits me. It tells fibs. It trivialises history. And it is written in shoddy English. I shall burn it.

And if the motoring association sends me any more biblical nonsense to try to sell me insurance I shall direct them to the last eight words of Ecclesiastes 9:11.

Tat

Poor Mr Lee Williams. Mr Williams is 23 years old and he lives in America. America is a nice place and Mr Williams is young so he should be happy but he is sad.

One day Mr Williams went to a place where people write on you for money and what they write doesn't come off. The place he went to was called Eternal Tattoos. Eternal means that what they write on you really seriously doesn't come off.

Lots of people have tattoos. Most of these people are boys. Some girls have got tattoos but my mum says they are not nice girls and I should not talk to them, even when they talk to me. My mum says that good girls don't have tattoos because good girls have got more sense.

Anyway, Mr Williams isn't a girl. He is a very tough man. The trouble was that lots of people didn't know how tough he was so Mr Williams wanted to get a tattoo which would tell them. Then he wouldn't have to bash them up all the time. He could just show them his tattoo and they would say, 'Ooooh you're tough, Mr Williams,' and he would say, 'Yes.'

So Mr Williams went up to the nice man in Eternal Tattoos and said, 'I would like a tattoo which tells people I am tough.' The nice man said that all tattoos told people you were tough and what tattoo did Mr Williams want. Mr Williams thought a bit and he said, 'I want you to write VILLAIN on my arm.'

'Okay,' said the tattooist.

Mr Williams was happy because he knew that the word VILLAIN would frighten people. If he went into a bank he could just roll his sleeve up and point at his tattoo and people would say, 'After you, Mr Villain,' and let him go to the front of the queue. And if he wanted to buy something in a shop he could ask the price and when the girl in the shop said a big price Mr Williams could point at his arm and say a small price and the girl would say okay.

When Mr Williams came out with his new tattoo on his arm he was very proud. The first thing he did was to go into a clothes shop and buy a dozen T-shirts with nice short sleeves. He put one of the T-shirts on then he went up to an old lady in the street and he showed her his tattoo and said, 'Grrrr'. The old lady opened her handbag and took out her glasses and put them on. Then she started laughing. 'Ha ha,' said the old lady.

'Grrrr,' said Mr Williams again very loudly, but the old lady laughed and laughed.

'Stop laughing,' said Mr Williams. 'I'm a VILLAIN.'

'No you're not,' said the old lady. She was wiping tears from her eyes. 'You're a VILLIAN.'

Mr Williams looked at his arm and the old lady was right. He was a VILLIAN. Mr Williams sat down in the road and started crying. 'Boo hoo,' said Mr Williams, 'I wanted to be a VILLAIN.' 'There there,' said the old lady, and she put her arm around him and gave him her hanky to blow his nose. 'Don't worry about a silly old tattoo,' she said. 'I bet you're really a very tough villain indeed.' She was a very nice old lady.

Mr Williams went back into the clothes shop with his arm behind his back and he swapped the dozen T-shirts with short sleeves for a dozen T-shirts with long sleeves and then he went home to be sad.

But the story might still have a happy ending because Mr Williams lives in America which is a place with lots of lawyers. One day a lawyer heard about the tattoo that was spelt wrong and he went to see Mr Williams. 'I am a lawyer,' said the lawyer.

'I am a villain,' said Mr Williams, carefully covering up his arm. 'I break the law.'

'Don't be silly,' said the lawyer, 'the law is your friend. We will sue the nasty tattooist.'

'Oooh, what a good idea!' said Mr Williams, and the nice lawyer wrote a letter to Eternal Tattoos and asked for $25,000. The lawyer said it was for 'distress and embarrassment'.

My mum told me to say that there is a moral to this story. She said that most tattoos are a form of infantile wish-fulfilment which gratify a desire to render a temporary condition permanent, and to turn a hope into a truth. Furthermore, said my mum, tattoos reflect a primitive voodoo faith in the potency of words and symbols. This particular story, she said, illustrates human hypocrisy, the insincerity of rebellion, the universality of greed and the absurdity of the law.

I don't understand any of that. I just feel sorry for Mr Williams. I hope he gets his money.

Things

G od knows what I was thinking of, but today I bought a thing, an ornamental thing. The end can't be far away now.

Yes, I know, there's enough hell to be had with people, let alone things, what with the advertising bore and the real-estate bore and the talkback bore and the rugby megabore and the financial adviser whose advice ought to be to become a financial adviser because it is the only job he has ever held down and it has made him rich, but even these unspeakable people have one virtue which things don't have. Even though these people may keep me from the drinks trolley with their jokes off the Internet and their slip-on shoes and their undissuadable self-regard, and even though they may corner me and lecture me until my brain is molten with rage, I am consoled by the knowledge that these people will be somewhere else tomorrow.

Not so with things. Things are worse than people. Things are the real enemy. Hold a good messy party and however messy the people get they will at least go away in the end and clean themselves up. Things won't. Ashtrays, bottles, plates, discarded clothing, stains and sticky furniture will wait patiently through the night to greet you in the horror morning like the claws of conscience.

The only language things understand is violence. 'Never underestimate,' says an Owen Marshall character, 'the perversity of objects,' and in one of the most gratifyingly violent scenes in world literature he takes a crowbar to a malfunctioning pump.

Don't acquire things. Things fill the house and shrivel the soul. Who amongst us has not got a cupboard of things that were thought once to bestow ease and wonder on our lives but became dump-fodder within days? Bread makers, miniature vacuum cleaners, data days, exercycles, solar-powered shoe trees, all of them now standing in mute testimony to our acquisitive folly, our possessive myopia, our desperate yearning for a better world.

Once upon a time we were kids at Christmas who couldn't sleep for the excitement of being given things. But then we unwrapped the things and instantly discarded the things and started looking forward to Christmas again. And we remain kids at Christmas, but nobody loves us any more so we have to buy ourselves things and it still doesn't do the trick.

The worst of the lot are ornaments. There comes a day in the offal pit of disappointment known as middle age, when you attend a Sunday market and in among all the tosh and garbage, the home-pickled vegetables, the unidentifiable bits of used plumbing, the cracked crockery, the Complete Home Handyman 1971–74 bound in genuine leatherette, you find a pretty something and you finger the pretty something and the woman in the coat looks up and senses weakness and says it's rather nice, isn't it? You ho-hum non-committally but the ghastly blank of home is shouting to you that it would look nice on the mantelpiece and it's only $9 and, well, it's just like that moment when you stop at the top of a particularly steep bit of ski slope and you peer over. Streams of children ski past you and over the cliff with a whoop, so finally humiliation launches you off the edge with a dread in your throat and a lump in your heart and after that it's just gravity and terror. Same with ornaments. Buy one and you're a gone possum. You've entered a world without limits, a world of china dray horses, cats in brandy balloons, landlady paintings of lolling senoritas and commemorative Charles and Di plates.

I know. I've done it. The rest home looms.

Smile at the nice axe-murderer

California has given us a new hero. Most Californian heroes are artificial and implausible media creations – Mel Gibson, Leonardo di Caprio, Ronald Reagan – but this new hero is of an earthier nature.

Her name is Richelle Roberts and she works as a produce clerk in a supermarket in Martinez, California. I presume this means she builds pyramids of tomatoes, and plasters them with those informative stickers which tell you that what you have just picked up is a tomato. And perhaps Richelle Roberts longs for Mel Gibson to wheel a trolley up her aisle so that she can slip him a pomegranate. Anyway it sounds a pleasant life.

But Richelle Roberts is unhappy, and not just because people keep asking if her name is a spelling mistake. She is unhappy because men who are not Mel Gibson keep accosting her at work. They bail her up against the apricots and tell her she's a peach.

Nor is Richelle the only one to be accosted. Eleven other women at this supermarket share her feelings. So tired are they of hiding behind watermelons to avoid the attentions of men who are not Mel Gibson that they have filed grievances against their employer, the Safeway supermarket chain.

The cause of all this unhappiness is the company's 'Superior Service' policy, according to which employees are required to 'anticipate customers' needs, take them to items they can't find, make selling suggestions, thank them by name if they pay by cheque or credit card, and offer to carry out their groceries.' Above all they must 'smile and make eye contact.'

Thus if an axe-murderer out on parole for good behaviour – how can one behave badly in prison? – asks Richelle what's hot in fresh fruit, Richelle has to gaze into his troubled eyes, smile, pack

35

pawpaws into a bag for him and carry them out to the boot of his car. If Prince Charming then happens to bundle Richelle into the boot with the pawpaws and drive her off to the trailer park to practise his cleaver work, that, as they say, is tough bananas. While he hacks at her limbs the Superior Service policy requires Richelle to look him in the eye and ask if he is having a nice day.

What we're dealing with here, of course, is marketing. It used to be called selling. Door-to-door salesmen since time began have practised the big smile and the glad eye. It makes the customer feel liked. Being liked arouses the happiness gland and the happiness gland opens the wallet.

One of the most distinctive qualities of salesmen, however, is that most of them are men. By and large men are bigger and stronger than women. Furthermore, salesmen have always been free to smile or not to smile. Richelle Roberts and her colleagues do not have that choice.

If a woman looks a man in the eye and flashes the sort of teeth that only the Americans seem to manage, a man tends to feel very good indeed. All sorts of testosteronic things surge through his veins. Too many men fail to master testosteronic things, which is why Richelle Roberts finds herself up against the apricots more often than she would wish.

Well, Richelle Roberts has had enough. She insists that she should decide for herself 'who I am going to say hello to with a big smile.' But the management of Safeway thinks differently.

The spokeswoman for Safeway is called Debra Lambert, which confirms suspicions about Californian spelling. Ms Lambert admits that since January the company has been sending 'undercover shoppers' into its supermarkets. If Richelle and her colleagues don't smile at the secret agents they receive 'negative evaluations'. 'Negative evaluations' lead to 'remedial training'. Any failure to be remedially trained can lead to that altogether simpler thing, the sack.

Spokeswoman Lambert admits that 'sometimes customers get out of line' but she doesn't see it 'as a direct result of our initiative'. By 'initiative' Ms Lambert means the Superior Service policy.

As so often the problem lies with words. Debra Lambert is bound to be in the wrong because she can say 'negative evaluations' and 'remedial training' without throwing up.

But the nub of the matter is in the word 'service'. What Safeway calls service is not service. Service is courtesy, politeness, attentiveness, thoughtfulness. It is the recognition of a relationship between seller and buyer.

Eye contact and a flash of teeth denote a relationship not between seller and buyer, but between people as people. The eyes and the mouth signal personal interest. Richelle Roberts is employed to sell fruit and vegetables, but the Superior Service policy requires her to sell herself.

In short, Safeway hired a person but, in order to make more money, they wish her to become a retail whore. They wish her to use body language to tell lies. Richelle Roberts is fighting, not for the freedom to be discourteous or inattentive, but for the freedom to be honest, to be herself. It is a cause worth fighting for.

Hot Christmas

Nine o'clock on the morning of Christmas Eve. Though clouds like Santa's beard fringe the Port Hills, the day bodes hot. I have to go to town for I have two presents still to buy and, besides, the shops will be shut tomorrow. I have a fridge full of groceries but I fear the shutting of shops as Neanderthal man must have feared winter.

In Linwood Avenue the asphalt shimmers and the trees are heavy with leaf. Outside a derelict gate near the gang headquarters a little boy and a little girl wave to cars. She waves a bottle of orange drink. He waves a little purple windmill. I wave back. The children don't notice. The radio is playing 'Good King Wenceslas'. As the page plants his feet in his master's footsteps in the snow, I put on my sunglasses.

Parking in town is a joy, but I can find nowhere to do it. A shaven-headed man in a ute steals the park I had waited for. I congratulate him with my horn and drive away before he gets out.

The multi-storey car park claims not to be full. After a cheerful encounter with the ticket machine which is just beyond reach, I do a neat hill start on the ramp which does no significant damage to the car behind me.

The giant yellow grasshopper leg lowers, the friendly voice of the radio fades into static and I'm ingested by a world of concrete, white arrows, red notices and nobody.

All parks on lower floors are reserved for senior members of the administration of the Department of Facelessness. The parks are empty, but if I park there I will be shot.

The building replicates itself endlessly. All sense of identity and place evaporates in the mesmeric repetition. Doubts blossom. What happens if I reach the top of the building and there are no parks? Is there a top to the building at all, or is it like Einstein's space loop constantly returning me to where I have been? The car park resembles a novel by Kafka.

Somewhere near the sky the building relents, and I squeeze between a Saab and a concrete pillar. The pillar is decorated for Christmas with paint from the doors of previous cars.

The stairwell is decorated with ancient black chewing gum and has been freshly sprayed with eau de pissoir.

I emerge into the street to a shock of sunlight. Shoppers throng. The easterly bounces the sun off the plate glass windows. Above the shopfronts the Edwardian bricks and window arches look as old as morality.

I have no gift for gifts. In the shops I find a plethora of gaudy, tawdry things that do not sing as I would want my gifts to sing. I find flying-pig bottle stoppers and dog-biscuit boxes that bark and models of the Teletubbies and the *Bumper Book of Jokes* about Auckland.

If we buy a lot of the tawdry, gaudy things it is called a good Christmas. Confidence rises and the economy swells. By filling our houses with tat we haul the country out of recession. It is called growth and it is called success and it is called happiness.

In Cathedral Square, a man tries to sell me a fish for $150. The fish comes from Wyoming, is set in stone and is several million years old. The fish is older than Christ. I resist it.

The cathedral squats in a Victorian sulk. It has lost the battle for Christmas. From the stalls that sprawl at its feet I buy a green dish and a bracelet and I feel I have done well.

Retrieving the car from level 13b, I drive to the supermarket and miraculously find a park, despite the man in the white coat who tries to direct me the wrong way. The place thrums with people who do not smile. I haul a trolley from the trolley snake, battle through the fruit and vegetables, realise in the butchery that I have forgotten to buy carrots and I turn around. A phalanx of shoppers rolls towards me, their trolleys shoulder to shoulder, their faces set with the grimness of a retail Christmas. In the belly of my own trolley sits a bunch of asparagus.

> The world is too much with us; late and soon,
> Getting and spending, we lay waste our powers.

I can live without asparagus. I ditch the trolley, muscle through the phalanx, climb the turnstile and find my hot car.

When I emerge from the Lyttelton road tunnel I see that on the hills above Diamond Harbour the heat has melted Santa's beard.

Lying doggo

My dog ran down the drive after a cat and hit a car. The impact bowled him twenty metres down the road. His thigh bone was smashed to pieces.

When twenty years ago I broke my leg, there may have been a couple of Mongolian peasants who didn't hear about it but I think I let everyone else know. My screams split the sky and, in the days that followed, the fading echo of those screams was replaced by the gentle sloshing sound of a young man wallowing in self-pity.

Not so the dog. He whimpered, more it seemed from bewilderment than pain. When I reassured him he fell silent and merely trembled.

The vet doped him so strongly that the dog didn't even notice when I left him lying on a synthetic sheepskin on a floor that smelt of disinfectant. On the operating table the following morning the vet reassembled the pieces of bone and held them together with a system of metal rods and clamps, most of them sitting outside the leg. I saw the X-rays. I thought the reconstituted leg looked haphazard, too jumbled to knit into strong new bone, but I didn't say so.

The X-ray was easier to look at than the leg itself. It was shaved, angry, bloody, taut and hugely swollen. It looked like what it was, a piece of damaged meat, a condemned leg of lamb, a vast and putrid ham, a dead thing.

The dog was too weak and drugged to stand but he moaned when I left him. I drank sedatives myself that evening but slept fitfully. My mind conjured images of suffering.

I picked him up the next day. When I arrived his tail thumped the linoleum. He struggled onto three legs, leaning against a plastic cage and panting. When I went to the till to pay he whimpered and hobbled after me.

In the car park he smelt out my car. I had a towel to wrap under his belly to lift him onto the back seat but he needed no help. Back in a familiar place he whined gently with what seemed both pleasure and pain. I wound the window down. He stuck his face into the rush of passing air in the ancient manner of dogs and fell silent.

I dreaded having to help him up the steep and sharp-edged concrete steps to my house but I need not have worried. His lust for home drove him up them in a supercanine effort, dragging his useless leg like a sack of offal. My other dog nuzzled and licked the wound. The cat cautiously toured him.

He checked the familiar details of the house and he saw that it was good and he drank a bowl of water and I swear that he sighed with relief. Then he lay down to get better.

It is now five days since I brought him home. In that time he has uttered no complaint except when the cat batted a ping-pong ball around him. Even when he tried to climb onto the sofa and crumpled backwards onto the floor he merely yelped a single involuntary yelp.

The leg remains useless. Thin, bloody fluids have leaked from it and he has licked them away. He has cleaned every wound a hundred times. The plum-coloured anger has drained a little from the outside of the leg but the inside of the haunch remains as bruised as a tropical sunset. On the shaved skin a grizzle of hair has sprouted, like the first awakenings of a spring crop.

I am confident he will recover.

Far more significantly, so is he. In the last half hour I have battled to pin down in words what it is that I find so touching and admirable in my dog's manner. It is something to do with acceptance and faith, with trust and modesty. Patience seems to be the key word, derived from *patior* which means to suffer. I have sought the exact words but I have not found them.

And then a woman rang from Ashburton and we nattered of this and that and dogs and literature and for some reason a passage of Whitman came into my mind and it says all I want to say.

I think I could turn and live with animals, they're so placid and
    self-contained,
I stand and look at them long and long.
They do not sweat and whine about their condition,
They do not lie awake in the dark and weep for their sins,
They do not make me sick discussing their duty to God,
Not one is dissatisfied, not one is demented with the mania of
    owning things,
Not one kneels to another, nor to his kind that lived thousands
    of years ago,
Not one is respectable or unhappy over the whole earth.

Thank you, Mr Rodgers

I had been thinking that management consultants did not read newspapers. I had been rude about them and not one had replied. But now Mr Murray Rodgers has stood up for his profession and I doff my hat to him.

Mr Rodgers tells me I quack like a duck, which is fair enough because I had said much the same about one of his fellow consultants. He also said I should play with my duck in the bath while the modern world passes me by. That's fair enough too. I enjoy as much as the next chap a bit of ongoing infancy simulation in a non-conflict aquatic cleansing environment, and as for what Mr Rodgers chooses to call the modern world, well I'm happy for it to trot on by as much as it wishes.

But lest we forget what we are discussing, I wrote to attack the language of an advertisement for the position of deputy principal at a local school. The job description announced that 'the appointee will facilitate the ongoing development of the school's future positioning, strategic, quality management and planning processes.' There was plenty more such guff. Mr Rodgers says that he didn't write this guff but that he could easily have done so. That's some admission.

I object to language like this because it says little, bears little relation to reality, is needlessly complex and aims to impress by that complexity. It can be boiled down to very little. For example in the passage I have quoted, the word 'ongoing' means nothing. If development doesn't go on, then it isn't development. And instead of 'facilitating development' why can't the appointee just 'develop' something? The reason, I suspect, is that it sounds less impressive.

The appointee will develop the 'school's future positioning'.

Well, he or she could hardly develop its past positioning, so let's cross out the word 'future'. If positioning means what it ought to mean then it will need a big truck. I presume it does not mean that, but exactly what it does mean I cannot tell you. I wonder if the author can.

From Mr Rodgers' article I have learned that 'strategic, quality management' means ensuring that the teachers teach well and that they contribute to making the school a happy, busy and harmonious place. These are laudable aims. They are also not new aims.

Mr Rodgers tells us that 'the way people behave in organisations has changed remarkably over the last ten years.' True, they now employ consultants a lot more than they used to.

According to Mr Rodgers, the boss should 'treat staff as equals rather than as lower-class servants.' Well, over the last twenty years I have taught in several schools in several countries. All but one boss I have worked for has respected me. My bosses have asked me and my colleagues for our opinions. We have had meetings and committees. They have allowed us to work independently, and acknowledged the things we are good at, and thanked us and been open to suggestions. They have not needed a strategic plan to do this; they have needed wisdom, modesty and humanity. The best principals under whom I have worked have been outstanding people.

The implication of this is that either schools are different from business organisations – and in some important ways they are – or that Mr Rodgers' wonderful new discoveries about the way organisations work are not so new.

Mr Rodgers tells me that no longer would a deputy principal 'bark at smelly art teachers' but would tell the teacher 'what his wicked ways are...how to fix them and what the consequences would be of not fixing them.'

Well, I confess to exaggeration in the words 'bark' and 'smelly'. I find jokes and emphatic words irresistible. Nevertheless, had the teacher smelt and the d.p. barked, it would still have been clear to the smelly one what he had to do to avoid another bark, and how a bark could become a bite.

And however strategic your plans, and however developed your school's positioning might be, art teachers will still arrive at school from time to time with hangovers because they are people.

The irony of Mr Rodgers' article is that he writes clearly. For the benefit of unreconstructed dinosaurs like myself he explains 'strategic planning' and 'performance-management processes' in words that I can understand. In doing so he shows these ideas to be simple, obvious and in no way revolutionary. I cannot speak of industrial organisations because I know nothing of them, but good teachers have been running their classes in this way for years and good principals, their schools.

Furthermore Mr Rodgers apologises for the blather. 'Our ability to match the English language to these changes in a clear and succinct way is still catching up.' This is flawed reasoning. For one thing, as I have said, Mr Rodgers manages to express himself clearly and succinctly in his article.

But more importantly he has misunderstood the relationship between language and thought. In rational matters like this, we think largely through words. It is not a question of the words catching up with the idea because, in the act of thinking, the words and the idea become one. If the words are woolly it is because the thinking is shoddy.

To put it simply, Mr Rodgers says that consultants have not got the words they need to say the things they want to say. Yes, they have. As Mr Rodgers shows in his article, most things can be explained simply. And that is how they should be explained.

My beef is with the language. Let Mr Rodgers and his fellows work out what they have to say and say it as simply as possible. If they did this we would often see emperors wearing the ideal clothes for bath time with ducks.

The man who ate death

It started with the toast. I laid before him a slice of free-range wholemeal and a sliver of fat-free spread. As I turned away to bear glasses of hot water to table 21, he called me back, indicated the fat-free spread and asked what it was. I told him. He pushed it away.

'Butter,' he said, 'bring me butter.' Just like that. The women at table 21 turned to stare but he didn't seem to care. 'And lots of it,' he added.

Well, service is my middle name. I would have preferred Gloria, but life wasn't meant to be easy.

From the boss I collected the key to the dangerous goods cupboard, fetched a pottle of butter and bore it to him at arm's length. The stench of cholesterol made me retch.

'What's that?' he asked, pointing at the side of the pottle.

'That,' I said breezily, 'oh, nothing much. Just the mandatory health warning, you know. Butter kills.' I meant it to sting.

He ordered two more pottles. The couple at the next table left the brasserie in a huff and a hurry. Lunacy disquiets people. The man spread the butter so thickly that he left tooth marks.

The women at table 21 began to twitter as birds in the Amazon jungle twitter when they have seen a tree snake.

The man seemed not to notice them. 'Bacon,' he said, 'bring me streaky bacon. And fried bread.'

No sooner had he spoken than a crash shook every table on the little patio as a woman slumped from her chair to the ground. Twenty hands rushed to her aid. The owners of the hands rushed after them. 'Is there a health professional in the house?' I cried but it was too late. With the words 'fried bread' on her lips, and a look on her face that will stay with me until the day I forget it, the woman went limp as old lettuce. She had sipped her last hot water.

We turned as one to stare at the man whose words had shocked a vegetarian fat-free heart into stillness.

'White bread,' he said, 'it has to be white bread. Fried in the bacon fat until it glistens to the core. Add goose fat if possible.'

Too numb to do anything else I relayed the murderer's request to the short-order chef. He blanched. He also steamed and roasted, but he did not know how to fry. I explained the process. I could see that it shocked him but in the best tradition of short-order chefs he drew himself up to his full four foot six and set to work.

Carrying the plate out to the patio I could feel myself gagging at the smell despite the mask that Occupational Safety and Health requires to be worn by all people working with fried food. Customers recoiled from me wrinkling their noses like boxer dogs. One woman's hand slipped to her breast and clutched involuntarily at a crucifix. A stout party in a yellow trouser suit fainted.

The monster seemed oblivious to the general horror. He calmly buttered the fried bread, heaped the bacon on top of it, showered the pile with salt, carved off a forkful, raised it to his lips and… I had to turn away.

'Coffee,' he bellowed at my back, 'coffee with cream.' I was glad of the chance to flee. By now, customers were scrambling for the exits but the news had spread and their way was blocked by ghouls who flocked to see the man who ate death. I battled through the horde.

He sipped the coffee and spat it. 'I want real coffee,' he barked, 'coffee with caffeine.' The crowd gasped. Several more matrons hit the deck like sacks of matrons.

I was past caring. As I made his drug-laden coffee I didn't even bother with the mask. Ambulance officers lugged out shock victim after shock victim. Television cameras arrived. A little man in big glasses offered me wads for an exclusive. I brushed him aside and took the coffee to the table. The patio looked like Passchendaele. By now the man had eaten and was reading the newspaper. He topped the coffee with cream, sipped, sighed, reached into his pocket, drew forth a cigarette and lit it. The stampede was instantaneous. In ten seconds the place was deserted but for a litter of corpses, some killed instantly by the smoke, others trampled in the rush. Silence.

'Thank you,' said the man amid the carnage, 'I feel better for that.' As he left he handed me a hefty tip. I burnt it.

Call me Kissinger

Like all careers in international peacemaking, mine began humbly with a trip to the supermarket. With the adroitness for which I am known, I passed through the sliding plate-glass door at the second attempt, and as I stood rubbing my elbow I beheld a man with the gold teeth and the leather jacket that denote in these parts a Russian trawlerman. He was trying to make himself understood to a checkout girl who cowered behind her scanner. He spoke no English, she no Russian, and tempers were fraying like the cuffs on my modish corduroys.

Just as in 1BC the people of Judea had no notion who was lurking off-stage in the wings of history, so Mr Russian Trawler and Miss Packyourbags were unaware that destiny had sent them a linguistic Messiah.

You see, I studied Russian at school. And how my classmates scoffed at the time. 'Scoff,' they said as one. 'Ha ha,' they said. 'Do you imagine,' they said, 'that Russian will be of any use to man, beast or you in the long years ahead? Do you imagine that there is any demand this side of Vladivostok for fluency in an archaic, inflected, Cyrillic language?'

'Da,' I said. That floored them. Up they picked themselves and off they slunk to their grim little utilitarian economics classes, while I flung my babushka imperiously over my shoulder and returned to my study of the language of Pushkin and Samovar.

That was twenty-five years ago. A quarter of a century I have waited to justify learning the thirty-three letters of the Russian alphabet, and taming my tongue to words like Zdravstvooeetye which means hello and explains why Yeltsin hugs people rather than greeting them.

Meanwhile, back at the checkout things had grown critical.

Russian eyeballs were bulging. Light glinted from gold teeth. Miss Checkout had mustered a glow to the cheeks which could have grilled a chop. Hearing about me the soft flutter of the wings of fate, I drew myself up to my full five foot four and prepared to intercede. In my mind I saw my schoolmates of yesteryear eating their words with a side salad of envy.

Russian sentences bubbled up from the swamps of memory, many of them straight from my school textbook: 'I have a yellow bicycle;' 'The fat man is wearing a striped tie;' 'My brother is fond of ballet,' and, though I would not swear to the source of this one, 'Why are you coming so quickly, Igor?' I recalled all the words to 'Kalinka', and the night I sang it at the Dunsandel War Memorial Hall and danced like a cossack. I can still smell the geraniums that the organiser of the function brought to my hospital bed.

Anyway, now was my chance to put my knowledge to use. I eyeballed Mr Russian Trawlerman. 'Zdravstvooeetye,' I said. Somewhere amid the frozen foods a pin dropped. Mr Trawlerman looked at me. Miss Checkout looked at me. He, she, I and time stood still.

'Zdravstvooeetye,' I said again and smiled in the manner of all international conciliators. It worked. Mr Trawlerman relaxed and unleashed a torrent of Russian. He clearly held some strong opinions which he reinforced with vigorous hand movements, several of which did not make contact with my flesh. He finished and leaned over me in a manner which made me unable to ignore what he had drunk for lunch.

'Da,' I said. Then, in case this seemed a little obsequious, I added, 'Nyet'. That was all it took. In that traditional Russian gesture of friendship and respect he spat twice on the floor and left the supermarket.

While all about me gawped, I nonchalantly wrestled a trolley from the trolley snake and went about my shopping as if nothing untoward had happened.

The other side of the fence

In a novel by David Lodge; but I can't remember which one and I'm damned if I'm going to look it up to get the details right ; getting details right is petty, retentive and prim, and, besides, details rarely tally with the purer truth of memory; a gaggle of professors of English goes down and dirty. Driven by gin and guilt they confess the titles of the great works of literature they have not read. *War and Peace*, says one and his colleagues gasp.

As the temperature goes up and the gin down, each strives to expose more thrilling ignorance than the other. The eventual winner is the prof of Renaissance Drama who has never read *Hamlet*. (Don't bother to write and tell me I've got that wrong. That's how I remember it and it'll do me just fine. Even if it isn't what Lodge wrote it's what he would have written if he'd thought of it.)

So, anyway, the profs shake off the layers of lies of a life lived badly, and thus do what we all long to do in the small hours of the night where the truth squats beside us on the pillow and nags us to come clean, to return to the state of innocence where what we say is what we mean, where we laugh when we are happy and cry when we are sad, where mummy knows best, rusks drop from heaven and where life is a naked romp in the sun and tomorrow doesn't exist.

Oh to fling off all the fibs and neuroses, the things we said to look good, the flatteries we let pass, each of them harmless in itself but building over the years into a shell that hardens into all we've got. (Yes, that's a quotation too, from by far the best of modern poets and and if you haven't read him, tough, you should. He pins us down like grubs in a display case.)

All this then to introduce the woman who confessed to me

today that she had never seen a *Star Wars* film. She felt, she said, guilty. That's what she said, guilty.

Rejoice woman, rejoice. Your guilt is but fear of solitude. You are suffering from the grief of the fat child who is last to be picked for a team. The grief of the loner, the outcast, the sheep trapped on the wrong side of the fence, desperate to rejoin the smug dumb herd. All around you stands the open world of possibility but you're desperate for captivity.

The wrong side of the fence is the place to be, always, and anyway, woman, you are not alone. I have never seen a *Star Wars* film either and nor do I intend to. And I shall tell you why. I have not seen a *Star Wars* film because I hate them. They're trashy seventies junk with special effects and I hate special effects more than I hate netball or Thai food or media liaison personnel. Anyone with a computer and bottle-bottom glasses can make special effects. They're like those ghastly kids at school who got extra marks for colouring in the title pages of their projects. Never mind that their projects had nothing to say. Never mind that they had culled the stuff straight from encyclopedias. Their projects looked nice, so they won. It's the same with *Star Wars*.

Did you not see the footage of the 'people' rampaging through store doors at opening time last week to do battle over what the world calls merchandise? Grown 'people' frantic for plastic swords that glow when you wallop them, and models of Darth Skywalker (stet, damn you, stet) with arms that actually move when you move them. Did you not see these images?

Boycott *Star Wars*. Go for truth, substance, beauty, independence, art that examines a life, that comes with no plastic merchandise, no sub-Neanderthal hype. Go read *War and Peace*, for God's sake. Then write and tell me what it's about.

All day long I'd deedle deedle dum

Once upon a time I liked this woman a lot. Then I stopped liking her. As soon as I stopped liking her she started liking me. Now she has sent me a chain letter. I don't understand.

This chain letter goes by the name of a Nepali Tantra Totem. It contains the famous Nepali Instructions for Life, which are the drops of pure wisdom distilled from centuries of thinking by monks in monasteries on mountains. There's some inspiring stuff. For instance, number twenty-six of the Instructions for Life: 'Read more books and watch less TV.' Or twenty-eight: 'Trust in God but lock your car.' Aeons of wisdom there. Number fifteen of the forty-five indispensable Nepali Tantra Totem Instructions for Life is 'Call your mom.'

If I send this wisdom to zero to four people my life will 'improve slightly', and presumably the lives of at least four Nepali moms will be enriched. If I send it to five to nine people my life will 'improve to my liking', as opposed to improving not to my liking. Nine to fourteen people and I will have at least five surprises in the next three weeks. Fifteen or more people and 'life will improve drastically and everything I ever dreamed of will begin to take shape and I will become rich.' Thank you, monks.

> If I were a rich man
> All day long I'd deedle deedle dum

That song is wrong. You don't have to be a rich man to deedle-deedle-dum. I deedle-deedle-dum all the time. For me deedle-deedle-dumming means staring at blank paper, walking the dogs and gawping.

Everyone wants to get rich. For most people that means winning Lotto. Every day throughout the country a million sentences begin with, 'If I win Lotto.' We imagine that winning Lotto takes the strife out of life and replaces it with deedle-deedle-dumming. So it does. That's the trouble with it.

Anyone who wins Lotto immediately buys a ranch house of hideous design and en-suite everything in Surfers Paradise – and no place with a name like that could be anything but awful – slumps into a Lazyboy and gives himself to pleasure. What he meets is truth. He sees stretching before him a succession of days of endless sunshine, empty beaches, Australian cultural experiences and hours of deedle-deedle-dumming. And deedle-deedle-dumming – otherwise known as wool-gathering, doing nothing, lazing, sprawling, enjoying yourself, thinking, giving up thinking for drinking, musing, giving up musing for boozing, longing for dusk, dreading dawn, having the whole commercial chocolate box at one's mercy and realising the thudding truth that chocolates are nice in anticipation but nasty as diet – is hell. In a matter of months the Lotto winner is pushing a bicycle round the central city, carrying bags of litter and talking to seagulls.

You need to be able to have everything that you want to realise that you don't want it, that the carrot which dangled in front of you and dragged you forward was a bad carrot, a carroty mirage. The Lotto winner ends up grasping the truth of dear old seedy Thoreau the hermit-philosopher of the American backwoods who pronounced – God bless his dungarees and his little house on the prairie – that happiness increases in direct proportion to the things you can do without.

And the morals that emerge are all the old morals, the time-worn, shop-soiled tedious truths of travel being better than arrival, of hope springing eternal in the garden of human delusion. Lotto equals chain letters, which equal, for that matter, communism, fascism, advertising or God.

I was supposed to forward the chain letter within four days. If I failed to do so, unspeakable things would happen to me. That was five days ago. Ha. But I still don't understand why the woman sent it to me.

The barber's pole is fallen

The barber's shop delights me with its ancient leather chair, a sturdy thing that could have come from clubs where wealthy men talk wealthy things with other wealthy men and where no women go. And round a proper barber's chair a proper barber flits, a man of middle age and great discretion, snipping hair from fifty heads a day.

Repository of gossip, Mr Snips can turn his words to any subject any man can want. He soothes the souls of men and grooms their skulls and sells them cigarettes, and 'was there something else, today, sir?' A barber's shop's a womb of men, a sure and certain refuge in a helter-skelter world where nothing is as once it was.

Although the vanity of men can crow as loud and high as cockerels, we middle-aged take little pride in hair. Our strands are few and thin and all we want is lightly up and down and over with the buzzing thing which looks to have been built for tiny sheep. Like gentle dentistry it is, a cosseting, a reassurance in a spiky world. It takes a mere ten minutes, then the softest brush across the neck, a little squirt of something fresh as flattery, the deft removal of the loose protective cape, the thin cascade of clippings to the floor, the brief exchange of cash, the 'thank you, sir,' the opened door, the *au revoir*, and then the windy street once more with tiny hairs beneath the collar itching at the spine.

But *O tempora, O mores!* I must sing a song of doom. For the barber's shops are withering, the ancient chair is cracked, and with it go the cigarettes, the Brylcreem, combs and comfort of the past.

In suburbs where the houses cost a lot, the barber's stripy pole's been taken down, and in his place has come a hairdresser, or worst of all a stylist. Where once the barber simply cut and talked he now does layering and tints, and other things I neither need nor understand. No longer is he Ken or Ron. His name is Gustave. No longer does he wear the sort of jacket favoured by the sellers of ice cream, but rather now he greets me in a shirt without a collar. Designer stubble laid across his cheeks, he runs a little empire full of basins and shampoos with foreign names. The chairs that fill this horror shop resemble office furniture, and furthermore he hires a mass of Traceys and Charlenes to cut my hair. They fuss at me and preen and pat and as the noble Digby Anderson observed, the Traceys do not talk to me of politics or sport, but make enquiries how I'd like my hair. I say I'd like it cut. They think I've made a joke. Then little Gustave trots across and drenches me in cappuccino breath, and wonders if perhaps a hint of bouffing here or gelling there might spruce me up and...

'Listen here, my friend. Atop this head of mine there isn't hair enough to stuff a mouse's duvet, and all I ask is that young Tracey gets the clippers out and treats me like a tiny patch of lawn. Just up and over, down and round the sides, a little bit of shaving at the neck, and I'll be off. And while she does the job she's free to talk of rugby or of politics, of boyfriends or of God, but never once is she to mention hair.'

That's what I want to say. Of course I do not say it. As Gustave plans the battle with my scalp I sit in smarting silence. Then Tracey tries to style and shape the hair I haven't got and then I rise and pay exactly twice what I once paid to Ron or Ken. I say goodbye to Gustave and I wander from the premises and then I turn and tap upon the window. And when the precious Gustave turns to look I place my fingers in among my hair and muss it up.

A pyrrhic victory, of course, a tiny self-defeating gesture of defiance to a world that's gone to pot, but worth it just to hear a stylist squeal.

Sing, baby, sing

Whenever I take a shower I think of Simon Monk. In 1969 in the hall at Brighton Grammar School, Simon Monk tested my voice.

He pressed a key on the piano. 'Sing that,' said Monk. I sang that.

'No,' said Monk. He pressed another key. 'You're singing this.' The note sounded familiar.

'Sing this,' said Monk. I sang this.

'Next,' said Monk and I slunk off into a splendid thirty-year sulk. For Simon Monk was wrong and every morning underneath the amniotic pleasures of the shower I prove him wrong. Cocooned in steam I pavarotti song on song which shake the taps and set the window rattling. The cat, whose delight in watching me shower makes it unique within the scheme of things, reverberates with relish. My repertoire is broad but every shower includes 'Mine eyes have seen the glory of the corpse of Simon Monk.'

But thanks to Monk I'm shy of public singing. The national anthem has me mumbling at my shoes. It's all the dirge deserves, of course, but this is no world to hide virtues in.

But then came Mr Asia. He moved into the port in which I live and just to taunt me he opened up a bar, a little bar with cheap formica tables, beer in cans, a woman out the back who fries the prawns and, hanging from the roof, a karaoke screen. His clientele is mainly men from foreign lands who fish for squid.

I steered well clear of Mr Asia's karaoke joint until last Saturday, when Jon and I foregathered at the great Volcano, a restaurant awash with stars from Access Radio, and where the corks go pop till late into the night. We ate two plates of kidneys soaked in sherry and then set out to patronise a bar or two, and somehow as we walloped down the street we found our way to the forfended place where Mr Asia welcomed us with arms as broad as Christmas. A group of Portuguese made room for us, a small Korean sailor gave us prawns, we bought our cans of beer, then someone shoved a mike into my hand and asked if I would sing.

O Simon Monk, I thought, where are you now? You've held my life in thrall for thirty years, you've squatted on my neck and crushed my soul and how I hope you do a dreary job. I hope you check accounts for companies that manufacture surgical appliances. I hope you wear a dark-brown suit and live in some depressing suburb always under cloud. I hope you own a shelf of Swedish books.

For now my time had come. 'Oi, Mr Asia, play "The Green Green Grass of Home".'

The oriental version of the song went far too fast. My old house was still standing while the screen was stepping down from the train. I shut my eyes and carried on. And then, somehow, and somewhere deep in my neurosis, a blockage burst and through the breach came flooding notes as rich as velvet. I was transported. Passion poured from me, a great forbidden river of emotion. As I drew out the final notes I raised my hand to fend off the knickers that the woman who fried the prawns was sure to throw at me. I opened my eyes.

Jon was laughing, the Koreans were bent over their prawns, the Portuguese had gone, and on the screen the video was halfway through 'Delilah'. Mr Asia was applauding, but then he owns the bar.

I handed him the mike and toddled home to bed, the shade of Simon Monk a yard behind me, his footsteps keeping time with mine and muttering the words of Samuel Taylor Coleridge:

> Swans sing before they die – 'twere no bad thing
> Did certain persons die before they sing.

Back to the beach

A few million years ago, our forebears hauled themselves out of the sea and lay panting on the beach. And every year, at around this time, we go back there to do the same thing. It is a pilgrimage.

The beach is elemental. Earth meets water, water meets sky, and in the sky stands fire.

Few things live on the beach. The sand is strewn with the translucent bodies of little jellyfish which pop when you tread on them. Gulls prey on the shells and crabs that didn't make it back. Between the fertility of the sea and the fertility of the land, the beach is a barren strand.

And yet, despite the sunburn and the insects and the sand in the sandwiches, year after year we return to the beach, and we lie on the sand and we turn to the heat and the light like reptiles. Toes and bodies snuggle into the sand's warmth, for the beach is a sensual place. It is a place of flesh.

Little children sport in the shallows, naked as birth and squealing. They build things of sand, they fight and they bury their fathers. They will spend the rest of their lives doing much the same things.

It is the teenagers who are most in harmony with the beach. They parade lean, taut bodies and shriek together in the surf and play sex games in thigh-deep water. Or else they wear wetsuits like a second skin and seek to govern the waves. Seen from the beach they look like seals.

Their parents look like walruses. Time has stolen their lean and taut and replaced it with something that sags. No longer can they play volleyball or sex in the shallows, so they wade out deeper, rising on tiptoe with each swell of water to delay the moment that shivers the crotch.

Then they plunge, swim a few strokes and become instantly bored, for the sea is no good for swimming. There is nothing to hold on to, and nowhere to head for but the horizon. Faced with the aimlessness of ocean, they return through youth and frisbees to the beach and collapse on a towel to ogle or eat sandwiches.

Those who are still older do not undress at all. They bask in air and sun like plants, or they totter to the water's edge to paddle with the very little ones in their own second babyhood.

Over the course of any year we accrete things which we consider important. We gain money, status and vanities. At the beach we take them off again. We may spend the year caring about sport, but the games that we play at the beach don't matter. The beach is good for us.

In this elemental, physical world, the High Court judge becomes an old man with bumpy legs. The youth whom he lectured becomes king.

The beach is the edge of the world. On the horizon a huge and tiny freighter is held immobile by the afternoon. A black dog bounds and barks through the wavelets. It is simple and happy. A gull arcs perfect on the air. Its mewing means nothing. Like the sun and the sea and the land and the air and the people and the dog, the gull is.

Dig it and dung it

Our society is sick. And, as many a social commentator has commentated, the reason that we are poor in both pocket and soul is that no one these days grows vegetables.

Back when a pound was neither a kilo nor a dollar but something so dependable that you could marry it, every dad had a yard at the back called the backyard where he grew peas, potatoes, parsnips, pavlovas, everything in short that modern man buys from the supermarket.

In those days of huge families Dad would come home from work in his braces and collarless shirt, and without even pausing to put trousers on he would be out the back pulling his carrots.

But not any more. As a child of the late twentieth century I suspect that I am typical. Not only do I not grow vegetables, I don't eat them unless they are disguised by salt, grease or, ideally, meat. By vegetables I mean, of course, chips.

On those more or less annual occasions when I crave green stuff I open a packet of frozen peas, take a good deep health-giving sniff and throw them away.

But, last week at that cultural melting pot The Volcano Cafe, I met a man who grows vegetables. He evangelised for vegetables. He carried soil samples around with him. He even had cauliflower ears. I made a little joke about those ears but he didn't laugh. He wasn't the laughing type. He was a priest, a pastor of parsnips, a reverend of roots.

Passing around soil samples from under his fingernails he preached the joys of horticulture. A crowd gathered. I listened and I was converted.

The moment I reached home I dived under the house to ferret out my gardening tools. In no time at all I had assembled a spade and a stick. The stick may once have been a hoe.

As every countryman knows the best soil lies under the tallest thistles. I selected a stand of thistles like a Scottish rainforest and set about them with a will and the stick. The stick broke. The thistles didn't. I slung my stick, seized my spade, turned my sod and dug the thistles in.

The dogs watched in mute fascination. Half an hour, a heavy sweat and I had no more thistles. Instead there stretched away into the distance a thrilling expanse of brown, tilled earth, as sweet as God made it, and almost a metre square. My vegetable patch. My direct line to nature.

Friable is the word. The best soil, friable soil, crumbles between the fingers like crumble. My soil was so friable you could have biffed it in with the bacon. It held worms so big the dogs barked at them. I sifted the good earth through my fingers and had visions of terrific carrots, triffid beans and marrows like nuclear submarines.

In the supermarket I wanted to buy every seed in the rack but at $2 a packet, two packets equalled my annual fresh vegetable budget. Nevertheless with over 800 lettuce seeds to the packet I realised I could recoup my money with a roadside stall – indeed at a dollar apiece I could turn a $798 profit – so I splashed out on the seeds of lettuce, carrots, beans and frozen peas.

In fifty-five days, according to the packet, I would have plump lettuce. That meant December 2nd. By December 15th my cup would run over with stringless beans. Carrots and peas would follow before Christmas. I felt myself blossom in pocket and soul.

Back at my market garden in a warm, vegetable-encouraging nor'westerly gale, I dug a little lettuce trench in the friable and tore open the foil packet with my teeth. Lettuce seeds are remarkably small and light. Several of them settled in the trench where I patted them happily down.

Back indoors I turned my diary to December 2nd and scribbled a note to myself to hunt down approximately 780 fat lettuces up against the fence to the south-east.

The carrot seeds were tiny too so I just planted the pea seeds and the bean seeds. To the untrained eye these seeds are strikingly similar in size and weight to actual beans and peas. They must be among evolution's errors. It would take a hurricane to broadcast them.

The carrots hit the soil the next day. I couldn't recall exactly where I had planted my other seeds, and, besides, the dogs had done a little digging of their own, so I just dropped the carrots in here and there and smoothed the plot.

That was three days ago. According to the packets none of the seeds should germinate within a week, but my friable is so rich that already I've got green things sprouting all over. I shall water them, nurture them, watch over them with a mother's care and then eat them. It's a wonderful world.

Underground heroes

When I opened the paper this morning the years fell away. Suddenly I was thirteen years old once more, a boy in shorts, bright of eye, weak of chin and with my torso already hinting at the musculature that was to earn me the nickname Podge.

It's all to do with *The Guinness Book of Records*. That book was the Bible of my childhood. Every night, in the swelter of my suburban bed, as the mosquitoes hummed and I hummed along with them, I turned the oracular pages of *The Guinness Book of Records* and I took its wisdom to my bosom.

Thanks to those long tropical nights, I can, to this day, recount a litany of records at the drop of a hat. Indeed, at the tail end of a dinner party only the other evening, a popsy dropped her hat and before you could say narcolept I had pinned her to the wall and was informing her, among other things, that the most poisonous creature on this planet is not a snake, nor yet a scorpion, nor even a talkback host, but a frog. To be precise it is the Colombian tree arrow frog.

I let her know – and I could tell she was fascinated from the way she kept looking over my shoulder – that 0.000000003 milligrams of the venom from a Colombian tree arrow frog will kill a horse. Her eyes bulged like those of the frog itself as I elaborated on the horrors of Colombian pony trekking.

In my youth *The Guinness Book Of Records* so obsessed me that I asked nothing more of life than to be in it. Then one night I read in its pages of a man in Minnesota, who had thrown a fresh egg, and of another man, also in Minnesota, who had caught that egg. The distance between the two Minnesotans was 156 feet. No egg thrower and catcher in history had stood further apart.

A scent wafted by me. I flared a nostril and caught the heady whiff of glory.

In those days there came no lapse between thought and action and in no time at all I found myself in the back garden with an egg. By the light of a winter moon I could make out the residence of Mr and Mrs Braddock, an imposing brick bungalow perhaps two hundred feet away.

The egg proved a splendid missile. Back in bed I basked in the knowledge that I had a record within my throwing range, and I slid into the bliss of sleep to the lullaby of Mrs Braddock's alarmed soprano and Mr Braddock's bass threats delivered in pyjamas to a wide and empty sky.

The following day I skipped the many miles to school with a song in my heart and a dozen eggs in my bag. I knew that I had only to recruit an egg catcher and fame was assured.

Colin Potts was not, perhaps, the most co-ordinated child at Brighton Grammar School, but he was the most easily bullied. So it was Colin Potts who spent his lunchtime on the school football pitch stationed some two hundred feet away from me, and it was I who wore my arm to a frazzle biffing egg after egg for Colin Potts to catch, and it was Mrs Potts who sent my mother a dry-cleaning bill that made her gasp.

All this, then, to explain the pang of memory that stabbed me this morning when I opened the paper. On the international pages stood the headline 'Briton lays down record.'

Mr Geoff Smith, aged 37, has found his way into the good book by spending four and a half months in a beer garden. Such a feat used to be called studying at university, but, unlike a student, Mr Smith spent those months 2.7 metres underground in a wooden coffin. Only a tube connected him with the outside world, a tube down which his friends and family poured food and encouragement and, on the 142nd day, a torrent of congratulation. For on that day he shattered the world live-burial record previously held by an American. Forty-one days before that, Mr Smith had broken the European record held by a Mrs Emma Smith, also of Great Britain. The coincidence of surnames between the former European-record holder and the present world-record holder is explained by the fact that Emma is Geoff's mother.

I don't know about yours but my heart swells. While you and I have maundered through our days, the Smiths have made something of their lives. They have seized fate by the throat and have wrung from it a place in the halls of fame. Something thunderously human inhabits the Smith spine, something great and good, and like me you will rejoice to know that Geoff has sired three little Smiths. Let us hope that the DNA remains vigorous and that one day we will read of the horizontal subterranean exploits of at least one of these three.

What suffuses the Smith soul is the same sterling stuff which drives one man around the world in a balloon, and another to the South Pole with only a cellphone for company. When I read of such derring-do, the years fall away like leaves and I stand once more in short trousers with an egg in my hand, a football pitch stretching away before me, a spattered Colin Potts a distant speck and glory hovering on the edges of my vision.

Go home

It is two in the morning. Lights illumine empty streets, the night shift on the wharf loads a ship with a giant crane and popular music pumps through the walls of my house. I can feel it in my feet and spine. Someone in the street is having a party.

I love parties but I do not love this party. I would like to sleep. I tried holding the pillow over my head. I burrowed beneath the duvet. I counted sheep, turned on to my right side and my left side and my chest, but the sheep carried guitars and the bed thrummed with the beat and I grew angry. I rose and padded naked to the deck. The warm night air pleased my skin but carried with it the news that we all live in a yellow submarine.

I do not want to go round and complain because I too have held parties. When the bank generously bought me my first house I invited people to help me warm it. I also warned the neighbours. One splendid elderly man was all tolerance. 'Go ahead, Joe, have your party,' he said. 'Get the young people round and have a good time. I'll just call the police.' He didn't, of course. He and his wife were among the first to arrive. They brought wine and a plate of scones and they stayed until midnight.

But now it is well past midnight and the dogs are nervous. They do not know why I have got out of bed and the noise unsettles them. They sniff the air and are ready to defend the house, but the enemy has no form. The larger dog whines in confusion.

> Come on, feel the noise
> Girls rock the boys

I can feel the noise. It brings to mind a fancy-dress party I went to last year in one of the nicer suburbs. I do not recall what I wore, but Dave the host dressed as the young Queen Victoria. It was an exact likeness, except that Victoria was a small woman. Dave is a lock.

At an early hour of the morning the noise-control officer visited. He was not a lock. He wore a sad uniform and a moustache that did not command respect. He never stood a chance.

Dave came swanning to the door, his tiara glistening, his make-up impeccable, his orange organza ball gown billowing behind him. He dwarfed Mr Noise-Control who gripped his torch tightly.

'Are you the host?'

'Darling,' exclaimed Dave, and he clutched the little man to him, lifted him squirming from the floor and planted a kiss on his cheek that sounded like one of those rubber things you use to unblock drains. The noise-control man went away and we were all happy.

But the noise-man was there because sober souls were sitting unhappy in their houses round about and cursing the noise, just as I am doing now. I suppose the definition of a good party is one to which you are invited. All others stink.

'Can you hear the drums, Fernando?'

I can hear the drums. I could jab wads of wet toilet paper in my ears but then I would not hear the alarm in the morning and I have to be up by seven.

It must be a middle-aged party for the songs are from the sixties and seventies. I recognise them all. For each of us, I suspect, popular music will always mean the stuff which played when our hormones ached. In the turbulence of youth we absorb words and tunes that time cannot erase.

In a play by, I think, Noel Coward, a character spoke of the potency of cheap music. He was right, because cheap music is primitive. It embodies the most urgent urges of our lives in rhythms which echo the beat of the blood.

Like certain smells, songs unleash floods of memory. Right now the Police are singing, 'Don't stand so, don't stand so, don't stand so close to me' and the song hurls me back twenty years to a dank garden in Fontainebleau where I was crouching drunk on a stone pillar among bushes. I was pretending to be a griffon. It had something to do with love. I can smell the smoke in the air of that night, feel the waxy texture of the leaves that brushed against me, sense the breathless all-importance of desire. The Police are now middle-aged and so am I.

It is three o'clock and I can hear guests leaving. They are loud and happy. With sentiment dripping from every word, The Seekers are singing 'The Carnival is Over', and I hope they are right.

Creep into thy narrow bed

Do you fret about apostrophes? When the menu says 'curry with vegetable's' do you froth?

Well, it is time to give up. Stop frothing. We've lost. The illiterates have won and it just doesn't matter. They have swarmed down from the hills with horns on their helmets and oaths on their breath, and they have ransacked the citadel, burned the library, ravaged the virgins, broken the necks of the vintage bottles and killed the little apostrophe. And they don't care. They care for their cellphones and their foreign bottled lager but they do not care for the apostrophe, and because they are so many and so heathen you might as well stop resisting.

> Let the long contention cease!
> Geese are swans, and swans are geese.
> Let them have it how they will!
> Thou art tired; best be still.

By their signs shall ye know them and their signs are everywhere: Egg's for sale; Hot Chip's; Womens Toilets'.

Using the apostrophe to indicate ownership is a modern convention. To be sure, Shakespeare used the apostrophe, but only to indicate a missing letter, just as it is used in other languages. When Shakespeare wrote St James's Street he inserted an apostrophe only because he had omitted an e. The possessive use of the apostrophe was unheard of before 1725 and much derided thereafter. But you and I know in our bones that when the possessive apostrophe dies, then civilisation will wither, and we will be left atop a heap of rubble and we will be left lamenting.

How fiercely we once fought for it. I smile when I recall how we mocked the shops that sold sausage's, and how we wrote ferocious letters to newspapers, and how we who laboured in the classroom expended gallons of red ink circling childrens and childrens' in children's essays and did not count the cost. But it has got us nowhere. And now it is time to give up. We have lost.

> Creep into thy narrow bed,
> Creep, and let no more be said!

The illiterates will tell you that we don't need the possessive apostrophe. They will say, if they can be bothered to say anything, that putting an apostrophe after an s to indicate a possessive plural makes no sense because no letter is omitted. They speak true. And they will say that we do not need the apostrophe to make our meaning clear because we get by perfectly well with the spoken language, despite the apostrophe being inaudible. And again they speak true, but there are greater causes than truth and the apostrophe is one of those.

Nevertheless the war is over and it is lost. Illiteracy has won the day. All you can do is to hold up your head in the knowledge that you fought the good fight and that your wounds are in the front.

> They out-talk'd thee, hiss'd thee, tore thee?
> Better men fared thus before thee.

But, in the end, what greater thing can a man do than stand and fight for punctuation? Though the apostrophe may be irrational, irrelevant, confusing, pointless, modern and wrong, a man can love it more dearly than he loves life itself. Do you, as you read these words, feel something that swells in the chest and stirs in the loins like a lizard quickened by the sun, something that goes beyond reason, something that says with quiet strength, 'I am and I believe'? You do?

> Charge once more, then, and be dumb!
> Let the victors, when they come,
> When the forts of folly fall,
> Find thy body by the wall!

Ant

I have always understood that bit in *The Rime of the Ancient Mariner* when the Mariner was becalmed. The sea had turned to slime and nasty creatures were crawling on it. The sad Mariner looked down on these creatures and

> A spring of love gushed from my heart,
> And I blessed them unaware.

I felt much the same way about my blue ant.

The ant landed on my hand while I was lunching on a focaccia sandwich. Focaccia is Italian, of course, and translates as a sandwich that costs too much. I don't believe the ant wanted the sandwich. More probably it mistook me for a flower. It is an easy mistake to make.

The ant bore all the hallmarks of an ant: three body segments, two feelers and six legs like flimsy filaments. But this ant had wings. The wings were cobalt blue. I had never met an ant with blue wings before. I showed it to John.

John plays the violin and is little known as an entomologist. When I pointed out the wings, he said 'very nice', which is probably as far as John is willing to go in praise of ants.

Either the ant was exhausted or it appreciated the warmth of John's praise, because it stayed. I ate my focaccia with the other hand. A woman called Jilly whom I had not seen for ages made to kiss me. I pointed out the ant. The kiss never landed.

I had an appointment in town after lunch and the ant came with me. A breeze had risen. For the length of Worcester Boulevard I shielded the ant in the manner of one carrying a lighted candle. The ant waved its feelers a bit, and the blue of its wings caught the sun, an electric blue that pleased me so greatly that I pulled up only inches short of a lamp-post.

I thought my ant might amuse Jill, the hard-talking soft-hearted receptionist at the publisher's. I climbed the stairs and pushed open the door which announces its opening with the sort of noise that precedes an incomprehensible public announcement at an airport.

'Hello, Jill,' I said, 'look what I've got.'

Jill was so amused that she knocked over a pile of invoices as she fled. From the back room she instructed me to 'get rid of it.'

'But,' I shouted, 'you don't even know what it is.'

I couldn't make out the exact words of Jill's reply but it seemed wise to heed the tone. Bing-bong went the door as I took the ant outside and blew gently on it to make it fly. It hesitated. I like to think it had enjoyed creating a minor sensation in a publishing house. Then it flew. I felt a pang of grief like a tiny blood-red stitch.

Back upstairs it took a while to make my peace with Jill. She had thought the ant was a spider. I can understand that. I too find it hard to cherish spiders. It is something to do with the way their legs arch and the body is slung between them. They remind me of the McDonald's logo. Anyhow, it will be many weeks, I fear, before Jill greets me again with any warmth.

In search of accuracy I have just rung a woman who knows. The ant was apparently most likely to be proctotrupid. That's a parasitic wasp. For me, however, it was an ant with blue wings, and I liked it.

Beat the beet

I'm going to have a silver beet party. You are invited. It's BYO. A few months ago I wrote of the intensive preparations that went into my vegetable patch. Clearly my return to the soil struck a chord, and many readers have since asked me how the harvest has gone. This column is dedicated to both of those readers.

Firstly, I believe in forgiveness. So, I hereby and publicly forgive the prankster who scattered the weed seeds. It was a good joke and in case he or she hasn't dared to return to check on his handiwork I can tell him or her that it succeeded. Rarely can so dense a crop of weeds have been raised in so small a space.

Baby weeds and baby vegetables are remarkably similar in colour, and I murdered many an infant lettuce until a horticultural neighbour taught me what was what. Thereafter keeping the weeds down became a simple matter of eight hours' hoeing a day.

The hoe is an entertaining little tool. Mine can skirt around a thistle for several hours, but give it the sniff of a bean plant and it will scythe the life out of it before you can say unprintable. I found, in the end, that the best way to weed was by hand, starting at the end of a row and working backwards along it, pulling out the weeds as I went and taking care to tread heavily on the vegetable plants behind me.

My first crop was peas. Pea plants have endearing little tendrils that grope blindly in the air, like the hands of orphan babies. I suspended a string above the row of peas and to that string I tied other strings, strings that swung in the breeze for the peas to seize. And the orphan peas that seized in the breeze so pleased me that I wrote a little poem about them which I shall spare you.

Three months after sowing I had a mass of fat pea pods which supplied me and the horticultural neighbour with evening meals for the whole of one Tuesday. All the same, I can tell you now that nothing compares with the succulence of a pea picked fresh from the garden, apart, of course, from the succulence of a frozen pea.

My dwarf stringless beans lived up to their name. They showed no hint of string and with the aid of a magnifying glass I gathered many a bulging thimbleful.

Lettuces flopped. I grew a popular variety with a crisp balled heart and flavoursome buttery leaves which goes by the name of Slug's Delight. With gratifying speed the lettuces pushed their buttery heads up through the soil, but each evening, as darkness fell over Lyttelton, one could catch on the wind the dulcet notes of a slug horn, followed by the steady trudge of the slug battalions. Down from the hills the slugs came rumbling, frolicking and tumbling, and they settled on my crisp balled hearts and my flavoursome buttery leaves.

The crunch of slug jaws was such that sleep was impossible. In the end I rigged up a little maimai where I would sit up all night with the dogs, brewing cup after cup of whisky on a little spirit stove and occasionally raising to my shoulder the ancient slug gun and firing blindly into the vegetable patch. The dogs would bound out to gather the corpses and lay them reverently at my feet, but the cause was hopeless. If you've seen the film *Zulu* you'll know exactly what I mean. In the end I ate only one lettuce and it looked like a string vest. Deep in its raddled heart I found a slug, gently snoring and sporting a look of beatific satisfaction. I tossed it on the barbecue, heard it squeal, watched it shrivel, laughed a hollow laugh and fed it to the dogs.

But all was not disaster. Graeme told me to grow silver beet. You can't go wrong with silver beet, said Graeme. Even a moron could grow silver beet, said Graeme. I wasn't sure I liked the tone of that last line, but in deference to Graeme I planted six silver beet seeds. And from those seeds came six strong plants which grew like a rainforest, their crinkled leaves swelling visibly, powering unstoppably skywards. My silver beet swelled into slug-shrugging monsters which dwarfed the dwarf beans, terrorised the orphan peas and shaded the deck. Of late the silver beet has taken to knocking at night on the window of the bedroom where the dogs and I cower together behind the chest of drawers.

Yes, the silver beet was a triumph, but I hate the stuff. It tastes of school cabbage. If you'd like some, please come to the party. BYO axe.

So, where are they?

I was reared on a television programme called *Tomorrow's World*. Raymond Baxter the presenter looked like an accountant but lacked the fizzing personality. On *Tomorrow's World* he prodded gizmos with his ballpoint pen and explained how they would revolutionise my life. I remember house-cleaning robots, self-steering cars and backpacks for personal flight. I wanted them all right then. But Raymond Baxter patted me on the head and told me I must wait.

The date I would have to wait for was always in the middle of the 1990s. The nineties defined the future. They were unthinkably distant. The nineties would bring ease. In the nineties all drudgery would be done by machine. The only industry would be leisure. The world would hum with technology. My job would be to wear a sort of thin purple wetsuit and loll in a hammock. Once in a while I would loll across to the orgasmatron.

In the brave new world of the nineties, the word labour would be obsolete. The dictionary would define it as:

i.   an activity indulged in by ancient civilisations
ii. pain suffered by women in a primitive system of reproduction
iii. the name of an extinct political party.

The nub of it all was the labour-saving device. Work was bad and leisure was pleasure. Never mind that people like work. Never mind that people dread unemployment. Never mind that people cling to jobs like life-rafts in the great ocean of pointlessness. Never mind that people love to grumble and work gives them something to grumble about. Never mind the wisdom of great thinkers like the bloke whose name I can't remember and can't find in the dictionary of quotations who said, 'He who chops his own firewood warms himself twice.' No, never mind truth, we must make people idle. By the time the nineties came round, indolence would be in.

Well it isn't in. As far as I can tell, people seem to loll less than they used to and work more, probably because they like it. Nor do I see around me the gizmos that Raymond prodded with his pen and promised me I would have. Nearly all the labour-saving devices that exist today, existed when Raymond was a mere gleam in his mother's oestrogen. And those same labour-saving devices still don't save labour.

Take, for example, my vacuum cleaner. I wish you would. It has the same brand name as a chainsaw but is much less fun. Nevertheless, when I bought it I thought it would be fun. I took it home, assembled its famously long wand – and why for God's sake is it called a wand? the only magic this machine managed was to make me part with $450 – plugged it in and got wanding. After two minutes, the dogs had gone crazy, my back ached and the carpet looked just as it always did. The only way I found to prove that the vacuum cleaner was working was to lay cat biscuits on the floor and race the dogs to them. Or else I took the thingy off the wand end and sucked lumps of my calf muscle. It was vaguely exciting. I also enjoyed, for reasons which puzzle me but might intrigue Freud, the little pedal that retracted the cord like a rattle-snake.

Otherwise the thing was, is and always will be a waste of time. The only dirt it picks up is dust and dust is good for us. Get rid of dust and people start getting allergies to things like mites and oxygen. Dust is also useful. I can never find a pen near the phone so I write notes in it. As far as I am concerned, anything that isn't big enough to trip over isn't dirt. And if it is big enough to trip over you can't pick it up with a vacuum cleaner. Quentin Crisp, whom I also can't find in the dictionary of quotations, said, I think, more or less, that there was never any need to do housework. After the first few years the dust didn't get any worse.

The only function of my vacuum cleaner and many another labour-saving device is not to save labour but to create it. First, someone has to labour to make it. Then, the buyer has to labour in order to pay for it. Thirdly, once he has bought it, the buyer feels obliged to do labour that he didn't feel the need to do before. And so the economy swells and feasts upon itself and the balloon grows and we all work harder and the century accelerates towards its climax and tomorrow's extraordinary world is nothing like the one that Raymond Baxter promised.

Perhaps we should be grateful.

Telephone technique

Using the telephone is a matter of technique. It starts with what to say when you pick it up. Some people say their own telephone number. This seems to me to to be about as useful as the Spanish '¡digame!' which means 'speak to me'.

I have experimented with greetings and found that an instant breathless 'Thank God you've rung' can start the conversation on a merry note. But it can also prove staggeringly inappropriate.

One way around the problem is an answerphone but that presents the difficulty of recording a message. Knowing that they are being recorded can reduce even the most fluent of speakers to zombies.

Some people leave messages referring to themselves in the third person. 'John Smith is currently unavailable. Please leave a message and he will return your call at his earliest convenience.'

People who don't want to sound like prigs plump for the conventional: 'We're sorry but we are unable to come to the phone at the moment.' This phrase conjures an image of the occupant roped to a kitchen chair by Mexican bandits, but its actual purpose is to make burglars think there is someone at home. This makes sense because all burglars ring up before burgling.

Many answerphone owners leave messages which establish their character. Some record lengthy passages of the music they most love. I find I rarely share their passion. Others tell a joke. This is normally very witty indeed.

From time to time I receive calls from beautiful women who are frantic to meet me. But they always ring when I'm out and the answerphone puts them off. I know they have called because they leave just a soulful sigh and the sound of a receiver being lowered.

I frequently answer the phone with no trousers on. This is

because my phone rings most readily when I am in the toilet.

If I am expecting an important call I try to bluff the phone by heading for the toilet, hiding behind the door and holding my breath. If this doesn't work I relent and sit down. As a last resort I lower my trousers.

Over the years I have found it difficult and dangerous to run to the phone with my trousers hobbling my knees which is why these days I just step out of them.

There is also pleasure to be had from answering the phone without trousers, particularly if talking to important people.

But often the phone call that summons me from the loo is not from an important person. It is from a firm which is currently in my area and which yearns to clean my upholstery. An effective response is to tell them you are sitting at home without trousers on and would be delighted to receive a visit from their representative. I haven't seen a representative yet. This technique may work better for men than for women.

In the late twentieth century the phone has become a complex technological device. I now do my banking by telephone. When I've just been paid I ring the bank just to listen to my money. It's my favourite form of phone sex.

My phone can also link my computer to the Internet. The Internet does not please me but I relish the noises the phone makes when it is connecting. It's like a drum and whistle band of Martian lunatics. Less pleasing is the fax noise. It reminds me of the dentist.

The acknowledged masters of off-putting phone technique are the large corporations. You wish to speak to Mr Blankface. A synthetic voice invites you to choose from a list of options none of which bear any relation to Mr Blankface. You can summon operator assistance by pressing the hash key. This presents the problem of which one is the hash key. You press the asterisk.

Having dialled again you hear all the options again. This time you press the noughts and crosses and the same synthetic voice informs you that all the operators are busy at the moment and, though they do value your call and have placed you in a priority queue, would you mind holding and listening to the Albanian

Greatest Hits of 1967 for twenty minutes. You smoke and doodle and feel sorry for the people in the non-priority queue. From time to time your synthetic pal pops back to keep you keen. Finally you reach Angela. By this stage you are angry. Angela puts you through to Mr Blankface.

'Blankface,' says Blankface.

Now is your moment. If you really have to talk to Blankface, go ahead. Much more fun, however, is to say, 'Sorry, I'm in a meeting,' and put the phone down.

It's all about technique.

Weird stuff

A brace of young Mormons visited me the other day, dark-suited, soft-spoken and both called Elder. My dogs rose from the sofa to bark but the two young men did not falter. I invited them in and they took off their rucksacks and perched on the edge of the dog-warm sofa. Then they quietly and courteously tried to make a Mormon of me.

Elder and Elder's first question was whether I believed in a supreme being. I said I didn't. Nevertheless they spun me their missionary patter.

All religious belief is irrational. That doesn't make it wrong. Love is irrational too, and so is laughter. Life without love or laughter would be a pallid thing.

Any man's religion is his affair and his alone, but if he tries to foist that religion on to me then it becomes my affair. He has become a door-to-door salesman and I am entitled to study the goods. The goods that the Mormons have to sell are weird and shonky.

In the Mormon Visitor Centre in Salt Lake City, Utah, a glass box like a vast aquarium holds a life-size model of the church's founder, Joseph Smith. A recording tells how in 1830 Smith was praying on a mountainside when lo, an angel of the Lord, one Moroni, appeared unto him. At this point a bright light illuminates the aquarium.

The recording explains how the angel gave Smith some golden plates with church rules written on them. Smith memorised what they said. This was fortunate, because by the time he returned from the mountain he didn't have the golden plates any more. Nevertheless, it is on those plates that Mormonism, aka the Church of Jesus Christ of Latter-Day Saints, is founded.

I asked the two Elders whether it was true that Joseph Smith had lost the golden plates.

'They were taken back,' said Elder.

I asked them if they accepted the theory of evolution. They said they did, but when I asked if we were descended from apes they said no. They believed, they said, in Adam and Eve.

'What, literally?' I asked.

They nodded. 'I guess we kind of believe in evolution *and* Adam and Eve,' explained Elder.

Mormonism embraces a welter of far greater absurdities than this, many of them sinister. Furthermore, it is a religion which preys on the vulnerable. Some Russian sailors are stranded in the port where I live. They have no money and are far from home. Elder and Elder told me with pride that this week they baptised one of these sailors.

Elder and Elder are gentle, credulous, serious, law-abiding people. They have given two years of their lives to rent a house in New Zealand and pad the streets in search of converts. People mock them, threaten them, abuse them. People like me challenge their ridiculous beliefs. Through all this, they speak quietly and if things get rough they move away and pray for their aggressors.

A society of people like Elder and Elder would be free of crime and violence. It would also be hateful.

The Elders and I parted amiably. In the windy sunshine I watched them climb the neighbour's steps. They had dog hair all over the backs of their black suits. I felt sad.

Country music

I first heard 'God Defend New Zealand' twelve years ago at Lancaster Park when Canterbury were playing Fiji. The pre-match entertainment had consisted of a man in a sheep's head. This roused the people to a frenzy.

Then the people sang, and I was thrilled to discover that I had emigrated from a country with a bad anthem to a country with a worse anthem. Since then, of course, 'God Defend New Zealand' has had the chance to grow on me. It hasn't taken that chance.

I am no musician but the tune that represents this young and vigorous country has all the youth and vigour of a pauper's funeral in Ashburton.

But it is in the nonsensical lyrics that this song excels. Typical of that nonsense is the line addressed to the God of Nations, 'Hear our voices, we entreat.' If the God of Nations can already hear our voices then there is no point in begging him to do so. If he can't hear our voices, then begging him to do so is like whistling a deaf dog.

The God of Nations is presumably the God who will sit in judgment on the nations of the world and 'shall separate them one from another, as a shepherd divideth his sheep from his goats: And he shall set the sheep on his right hand, but the goats on the left.'

Implicit in the song is the assumption that we are a virtuous sheep country and not one of the smelly left-hand goats. The trouble with thinking ourselves to be a virtuous sheep country is that every other country also sees itself as a virtuous sheep. A rigorous survey of the national anthems of the world has revealed that the number of countries who sing about their goatish failings is below the margin of error. In short, every country claims to have God on its side.

This is particularly evident in time of war. During the Gulf War, for example, George Bush suddenly came over all religious while Saddam Hussein was constantly banging on about the will of Allah. George's God, with the help of a few stealth bombers, won this one, of course, thereby redressing the balance from the medieval crusades when Allah's Turks repeatedly walloped the Christians.

My point is that calling on God to defend us is a pointless piece of rhetoric from another age. It is jingoistic colonial nonsense. 'God Defend New Zealand' should go.

Replacing it, however, will prove difficult. Few anthems exist that are worth imitating. The French have got a cracking tune but archaic and bloodthirsty lyrics; 'Advance Australia Fair' starts well but goes on too long; and if you want a giggle, study the text of the Star-Spangled Banner.

If a competition were held to write a new anthem, I guarantee that the winning song would concentrate on ethnic diversity, sexual orientation and wheelchair access, and be quite unsingable.

So I propose a radical change, a change that would distinguish us from every other nation of the world. I propose a national anthem that everyone can sing, that inspires thoughtfulness, that demonstrates self-discipline, that encourages us to remember those who have gone before us, and that tells no patriotic fibs. I propose that we replace 'God Defend New Zealand', officially and permanently, with a minute's silence.

It would make a splendidly menacing start to a test match.

Hoonsville

A nger writes these words.

A car has just screeched up the road. Its noise made me shudder, the cat hide and the dogs bark. In the car's wake three young friends of the driver are kneeling in the manner of Muslims at prayer. They are sniffing the asphalt for the tang of burnt rubber. It excites these young men.

When I say young men I wouldn't like you to form an image of young men. Instead paint a little mental picture of three lumps of slack-jawed, lank-haired, foul-mouthed flesh in offensive clothes. Render that flesh volcanic with acne and give it the brain of a gecko.

Such people mistake cars for manhood. Their cars have spoilers and stickers and they tune the engines to maximum decibels and they overtake me in tunnels and the noise makes my heart leap and I know anger. Anger and loathing.

I do not want to be angry. I do not want to loathe. But they turn me into a Colonel Blimp with a noseful of burst blood vessels who fumes with impotence and bellows for the return of national service and discipline in schools and capital punishment and then has another big gin.

Hoon cars house boom boxes which thump out bass rhythms that Neanderthal man would find primitive. These rhythms vibrate through car and road and spinal columns and render speech impossible which is as well because these young men are barely capable of speech and they are as familiar with consecutive thought as they are with Swahili. They are barely sentient beings. They react to rhythms and noise with the same complexity that single-cell organisms react to light.

How these people get the money to pay for their obscene cars I do not know. They are too brachycephalic to work and too craven to burgle. I expect their parents have given them a lot of money to go away.

I wish my dogs were savage dogs. I should like to unleash the dogs of war and watch the baby motorists as the hounds bore down on them and see their eyes widen with horror and watch them turn and squeal and run and see the dogs bail them up against the bonnets of their phallic cars. I would watch them gibber and lard as the dogs drew close and I would see their cowardly souls etched on their pasty faces and then at the last second I would whistle the dogs into sudden immobility and the children would melt with terror and relief and their knees would dissolve and they would slide to the ground and they would weep.

They are quite beyond redemption. When they grow up they will buy black T-shirts and quilted anoraks and they will like motor racing. They will flock to a Grand Prix as if it were a religious ceremony, and they will inhale the incense of fuel and rubber and thrill to the liturgy of engine roar which would numb the mind of anyone who had one. As the cars, plastered with such exciting ads for contraceptives, hurtle round a circuit that takes them back to where they started, the hopeless ones will hover at the bends and pray that one of their heroes will lose control and spin and toss and crash and die and bits of bodywork will fly and it will be on One Network News to delight the emotionally crippled who weren't able to get there in person because they couldn't read the road signs directing them to the track.

Or maybe one day the hoons will travel to Africa to watch one of those hideous rallies which take place in the innocent wilderness – the ultimate test of man and machine – and they will take photographs of a lunatic sliding his wheels in the sands of the Sahara. Meanwhile, Bedouin tribes will move across the skyline in stately camel trains and peer with wonder at the madness and decide with the wisdom born of centuries of long civilisation that if a motor rally is the way ahead, the future, the developed world, the democratic West, the technological age, then they will stick with camels.

What I don't understand about hoons is why the police don't

arrest them. For making noise. For being what they are. For sliding to the foot of the evolutionary ladder. For the good of us all. For making me angry.

Only now, of course, I don't feel angry. That's the purgative pleasure of writing. And the kids are just kids. They're probably all right underneath.

A Parisian pig

I love the 'Briefly' bits, the juicy single-paragraph items in the newspaper about something nasty that has happened to a foreigner who lives so far away that I don't have to expend any energy feeling guilt, sympathy or any of the other emotions that we're supposed to feel lots of but which aren't anywhere near as much fun as the real emotions such as anger, greed and delight at another's distress. No, the shorts are splendid because I'm free to chuckle at a Belgian decapitated by a frozen chicken, and frankly it's more good news like that that this country needs rather than the weeping and wailing and gnashing of ganglions over the fiscal deficit and unemployment and the decline of women's rugby league.

So when I read in the shorts this morning of a hunter in France who was killed by a stag which he was not unreasonably trying to murder, I thought ha ha and inhaled another spoonful of my Tasti Blueberry Crunch. But as I chewed, my mind slid back twenty years to a clearing in a forest outside Paris where stood a derelict caravan and a dirty little tent which belonged to Philippa but which I had borrowed to do a bit of solitary-adventurer stuff around Europe, the purpose of which was to get it over with as quickly as possible before heading home to tell people lies about it.

Well, courage has always been my long suit, particularly when alone in a tent in a foreign forest with night falling and the wind soughing in the trees and nameless things with grins and teeth flitting between branches, so I just curled in the sleeping bag, hugged my knees like lovers and went in for a bit of quietly courageous whimpering, alleviated by swigs from a plastic bottle of nerve tonic ordinaire.

Sleep seized me well before dawn. The next thing I heard was a snuffle-grunt. It was the sort of snuffle-grunt one doesn't ignore. Not for me the sleepy roll over, the groan, the slow ascent from the deep waters of sleep to the bright cold air of consciousness. Rather, my flight-or-fight response, which has always favoured the first half of the formula, rendered me instantly awake, eyes pricked, ears gaping and my body rigid as a tent pole. I also cunningly stopped breathing.

Another snuffle-grunt, huge, breathy and dissatisfied, sounded just beyond the opening of the tent. Then silence, bowel-churning silence. I slithered from the sleeping bag and inched open the zip on the tent. I expected to be rushed. Nothing. I eased my head out from the opening like one of the more cautious brands of tortoise and met, at a distance of approximately a metre, a wild boar. It had murderous intentions and tusks.

My options were several. I could shrink back into my tent and wait to die, I could run away through the forest clad only in terror or I could do the sensible thing and attack the beast, wrestling it on to its back and then sticking it through the heart with a piece of plastic cutlery. I shrank back into the tent.

The boar had an amusing sense of drama. It snuffled around the perimeter of the tent grunting. I could only wait. I heard it pause to plan its attack. From my rucksack I drew a notebook, wrote the date, left everything to mother, signed my name and felt my bowels stir.

Thirty minutes later I opened the tent. In front of me, no boar. Round the sides of the tent, no boar. I stood naked in the dappled green of a forest dawn, raised my arms to the skies and whooped with the joy of being alive.

Across the clearing a man was sitting on the steps of the derelict caravan. He held a handful of bread from which the boar was calmly feeding.

Safety

I am suspected of wanting to kill children. My means of execution is a deck.

Some months ago when I was briefly flush with lolly I paid an architect to design me a deck, and a builder to build it. Both did a fine job, so fine a job indeed that I am now bedecked and broke. One part of the deck has fixed wooden seating round its rim to create a conversation pit and there, over the last few months, I have spent many a summer evening with friends, dogs and gin and we have tired the sun with talking and sent it down the sky. In short, the deck is a triumph.

If, however, I am ever to sell the house, I need to be able to prove that my triumphant deck is legal. So I rang the council and they sent a deck checker to check the deck. He rattled its rivets, he wobbled its noggings and then he placed his chin between his thumb and his first two fingers in the manner of one engaged in thought, and he said no.

I said what, and he said no again and he pointed at the seating and said it had to go. Children, said he, could climb onto the seating, haul themselves onto the guard rail and dive to their deaths. I pointed out the cushion of unmown grass ten feet below, but Mr Deckcheck was unmoved. This was, said he, an unsafe deck.

I invited him to scour my house for children. He declined, on the grounds that, though I may be barren, my successors in this residence – deck checkers talk like that – might be fecund. They might spawn hordes of little ones all of whom would like nothing better than to climb onto the seats and fling themselves into the grassy arms of eternity. The seating, said he, was unsafe seating and it had to go.

I argued of course. I argued that anyone who bought the house could see for themselves the lethal seating and choose not to buy. I further argued that my garden, like everyone else's garden, was full of trees which children with a death wish could climb and tumble from at will. Deckcheck stood adamant, bolstered from behind by the immovable weight of bureaucracy.

If, I asked, I were to remove the fixed seating and replace it with seating which was not fixed but which stood in the same place and which incorporated little ladders to make it easier for kiddies to clamber onto, along with perhaps a stoup of holy water so they could make their final oblations before crossing the bourn from which no traveller returns, would that be all right? That, said Deckcheck, would be just dandy. Just so long as it wasn't fixed.

Therefore, I said, if I were to unfix the lethal seating, but leave it where it was, that would be all right too. Yes, said Deckcheck, it would. So I did, and it was. The deck looks exactly the same as it did on the day that the deck checker came and found it lethal, only now I have a pretty little certificate to certify that it is safe and legal.

And having given me my certificate, Deckcheck toddled off to wage his war on unsafeness. He set out on his mission to check every deck, fence every swimming pool, secure every seat belt. If he has his way he will fell every tree, drain every stream, lock every medicine chest and ban sharp cutlery. And he will build for us a country of such anodyne safety, that not one of us will any longer need to be responsible for ourselves or for our children. Deckcheck will care for us. He will eradicate chance, banish fate, and when finally we grow so bored that we fling ourselves from our collective decks into the everlasting night of nothing, he will mark the event with a nice, orderly little certificate.

Presidential Shakespeare

President Clinton has been caught with his trousers down and many of us have got a lot to say about it. Most of what we say is blather. But many dead people have also got a lot to say about it, and dead men tell no lies. Foremost among the dead is Shakespeare.

Shakespeare's best-known plays are his four great tragedies, *Macbeth, Hamlet, Othello* and *King Lear*. Of these, the first and last in particular illuminate the present shemozzle in the White House.

The nub of a Shakespearean tragedy is that a man – it is always a man – falls from a position of eminence to a position of far less eminence because of some fault in his character, the famous tragic flaw. That flaw tends to be a passion which overrides his judgement.

My summary is simplistic, but it suggests nevertheless that Shakespeare may have something to say about Clinton.

Though eighty years of age King Lear was childish, vain and autocratic. Rage seethed in his blood. He would allow no one to cross him. When Lear's daughter Cordelia refused to play his games he cursed her and banished her from the kingdom. After that it all went wrong.

Surrounded by sycophants Lear handed over his power. The yes-men and the yes-women accepted the power then broke their promises. Lear raged at them but found that he was powerless. Frantic with anger and impotence he ran out onto the heath.

There in the wind and the rain he went mad. In his madness he grew. He saw that he had been childish, vain and autocratic. He learnt that power corrupts and that 'a dog's obeyed in office'. He learnt that he was 'a very foolish, fond old man'. When finally reunited with Cordelia he knelt down and asked of her forgiveness. 'If you have poison for me,' said Lear, 'I will drink it.' In short he learnt humility and gained humanity. He learnt through suffering.

The story of Lear bears parallels to the story of Clinton. Each, it seems, was blinded by supreme power. Each sought to gratify his whims. Each was caught out and felt himself betrayed. Each got down on his knees and begged forgiveness.

But the difference is telling. By the end of the play Lear has lost all interest in power. He mocks human politics and the hypocrisy of government. Its joys have become trinkets, baubles, the toys of a child.

But Mr Clinton still craves those toys. Though he calls his craving a wish to continue to serve the American people, he is transparently clinging to his job. It is not a pretty sight. If Kenneth Starr had not caught him out, he would happily have lived behind the lies he told about Miss Lewinsky. The Lear who had suffered and learnt would not.

Perhaps the play that cuts closest to the bone of Clinton's case is *Macbeth*. Driven by vaulting ambition and a ferocious wife Macbeth murders his way to the throne. Having murdered he murders again. Once he has started down the road of treachery he can only career at increasing speed to the black bottom of the hill. His followers desert him. His wife goes mad.

Macbeth does not find the redemption that Lear finds, but like Lear he sees the hollowness of power without integrity. He feels 'his secret murders sticking on his hands' and his title

> Hang loose about him like a giant's robe
> Upon a dwarfish thief.

When Lady Macbeth dies, he sees that corruption has so soiled his life that

> …that which should accompany old age,
> As honour, love, obedience, troops of friends,
> I must not look to have.

In the end he is pleased to die. The throne means nothing. Indeed life is just a tale

> Told by an idiot, full of sound and fury
> Signifying nothing.

Once again the parallels with Clinton are revealing. Clinton has murdered nobody as far as I am aware , but like Macbeth his lust for power has proved unquenchable. He lies to retain power. He quibbles with the meaning of words to hide those lies.

> O, what a tangled web we weave
> When first we practise to deceive!

Now it seems that Kenneth Starr has unravelled that web. Mr Starr's motives do not matter. His inquiry has shown that power, as it has done to so many for so long, has made an ordinary man drunk.

All men make mistakes, but heroes learn from them. They grow from suffering. Clinton has shown no sign of growing. We will know when he has started to grow because he will announce his resignation.

For though Clinton's crimes may be lesser and fewer than yours or mine, they remain the crimes of an ordinary man. An ordinary man should not hold an extraordinary office. Clinton is no hero and he should go. If he were worthy of his office he would leave it.

Dancing with Destiny

C.B. Fry was the golden boy of the Edwardian era. By the age of forty-one, Fry had gained a first-class degree in classics, broken the world long jump record, played cricket and soccer for England and been offered the throne of Albania. In addition he was considered the best ballroom dancer of his generation.

Now, when I point out that I too am forty-one I think you will agree that the parallels between my life and Fry's are too great to ignore. Admittedly Fry may have got a slight lead on me on the academic and sporting fronts, and he's also nudged ahead in throne offers, but I believe that even old C.B. would acknowledge that on the dance floor I take some beating.

Picture me then, if you would, at the society wedding of the year in Christchurch, leaning against a banister in my treble-breasted mohair, the essence of suave. My eyes have that half-closed Lawrence-of-Arabia look which steals over me late at parties. In each hand I idly clutch a bottle of the host's champagne. Another protrudes from my pocket at a rakish angle. Around the ballroom women visibly struggle to resist my allure. It says much for the women at this wedding that all have so far succeeded. But as the evening wears on I can sense the throbs of yearning in their breasts like the pulse of subterranean music.

Only one woman has dared to address me. 'You've got soup on your tie,' she said. Words can mask the strongest feelings. When you are in tune with the female psyche you see beyond words. 'I know,' I said, and winked at her. She understood, gave a little nervous snort that bystanders might have mistaken for derision, and melted back into the throng, her vital signs a-flutter.

I tongued my tie, openly, arrogantly. It tasted fine. I lingered over it, sucking the last of goodness from the viscose-and-rayon mix with its understated Mickey Mouse motif. I was conscious of eyes flicking my way. I waited. I did not have to wait long.

Barely three hours had flown by when out from the dance floor came Destiny. Destiny wore a frock of shot silk. The bullet holes gave glimpses of flesh that would have sent a weaker man to his knees. A woman of substance, glowing from the waltz. 'Destiny,' I whispered.

'You're drunk,' said Destiny.

I have seen it so often, the way women conceal their lust behind abuse. I merely smiled my knowing smile and swayed to an ancient internal rhythm. I would let Destiny take her course. She eased the bottles from my grasp. After a brief and sensuous struggle I let myself be guided by her will. She unloaded my pockets of their burden, as symbolic an act as you could wish to see. When she pulled the bundle of the host's cigars from my inside pocket I could see she was impressed.

'Come on,' she said, 'let's dance,' and I allowed myself to be led to the floor, pausing only to trip deftly over a potted palm. Awe cleared instant space for us in the crowded marquee. The band was hard at it. I sensed the shade of C.B. Fry prodding me in the kidneys. 'Strut your stuff,' said old C.B.

Dancing, said George Bernard Shaw, is the perpendicular expression of a horizontal desire. It took only one waltz, which may on reflection have been a rumba, to convince Destiny of my horizontal desire. I did this by treading on her feet a lot. I think I may have drawn blood. There was no mistaking my message. I dance for keeps.

Words were unnecessary. Nevertheless, as we lurched passionately on the spot, Destiny would murmur little tendernesses into my ear. 'Ow,' she would murmur, or 'Try standing upright,' or 'Do you have to do that?' The other dancers may have been fooled. I wasn't.

Somehow when the dance was done Destiny and I separated. But it didn't matter. We had forged a link that no man could put asunder. Thirst and exhaustion took me first to the bar, then to a remote part of the marquee where gravity was strong. Curled in a canvas corner I drifted into a dream in which I sprinted to the sandpit, soared aloft and came to earth in Albania where I ruled the rugged people with autocratic benevolence.

Suddenly old C.B. was prodding my kidneys again. I rolled over and flicked open an autocratic eye. Someone had glued my tongue to my palate. An Albanian was jabbing me with the nozzle of a vacuum cleaner.

'It's all over, mate,' he said in fluent English. 'Time to go home.' I wandered out into the eerie light of a Christchurch dawn, hailed a cab and went home to sit by the phone and wait for Destiny to call.

The manager's mother-in-law

Dufftown lies in the heart of the malt whisky distilling region of Scotland, but it has only one pub, a pub which claims to stock every available brand of malt whisky. I do not recall the name of the pub, but let us call it the Lotsa Scotch.

In, I think, 1978, Dave Collier breezed into the Lotsa Scotch and said he would like a malt whisky. The barmaid smiled a patronising smile, gestured to the array of bottles and invited Dave to pick his poison. Dave said he would like a Glen Hoddle. At the time Glenn Hoddle was playing sublime soccer for England, lazy soccer admittedly, but with moments of genius which made up for every indolence.

The barmaid frowned and disappeared. She returned with an apology. They were fresh out of Glen Hoddle, she said, but had ordered another case that very morning.

I recall this story today because Glenn Hoddle has just been sacked as the manager of the English football team. His crime was not the loss of matches – if that justified a sacking then no England manager would last six months – but his belief, as stated to a journalist on *The Times*, that disabled people were being punished for their sins in a previous life.

Mr Hoddle picked up this idea from a Mrs Drewery, who, apart from being official faith healer to the English football team, also happens to be the mother of Mr Hoddle's girlfriend. In other words Mrs Drewery is only a ceremony away from becoming Mr Hoddle's mother-in-law.

The first question to ask, which I have so far heard nobody ask, is whether Mr Hoddle and his almost-mother-in-law are right. Is it true that disability is a form of divine punishment? Well, the idea of God dishing out punishments to those who displease him is as old as mankind. Jove didn't stint on the thunderbolts, and whoever was boss of the Greek pantheon was no pussy cat either. The Bible, too, is packed with examples of God's wrath, and there's no shortage of people who believe that AIDS is God's way of scourging homosexuals.

Although most of us these days are less explicit in our belief in divine retribution, we still entertain the idea in terms of a natural law. 'He got what was coming to him,' we say, or 'What goes around, comes around.'

Reincarnation has a similarly long history. Pythagoras the mathematician, whose geometrical theorem is still taught in schools because it has been proved true, believed stoutly in reincarnation. So do Buddhists. According to *Brewer's Dictionary of Phrase and Fable*, a Buddhist supposes that man has passed through many previous existences, and all of the sins accumulated in these previous states constitute man's birth-sin. This sounds to me remarkably close to Mr Hoddle's twaddle.

And twaddle it is, ugly, stupid, obvious twaddle. But I can no more prove it to be twaddle than Mr Hoddle and his ludicrous mother-in-law can prove it to be true, and in a civilised society Mr Hoddle and I are free to believe different things.

Except it does not seem that Mr Hoddle is free to believe. He has been sacked for his beliefs. Now if he were the Archbishop of Canterbury – and stranger things have happened in the Church of England – I could understand his being sacked, because an archbishop is employed to propagate certain beliefs. Mr Hoddle, however, was employed, not as a spiritual leader, but to coach football. I don't see what his beliefs have got to do with football. As the sage J.R.Mills has said, if a fitter and turner belongs to the Flat Earth Society in his spare time, that may mean he is nuts, but it doesn't mean he is a bad fitter and turner.

Mr Hoddle has been sacked because he has been breathtakingly politically incorrect. He has insulted the disabled. I am only surprised that he did not go on to say that black people are inferior to white people. Maybe, if he had been asked the right questions, he would have done so.

Because he has insulted the disabled, his critics agree that he is mad, bad and dangerous and that he should go. I do not dispute that he is nutty as a bag of nuts, but I do dispute that he is dangerous and that he should go.

His sacking implies not only that a man is not free to believe what he wants to believe, and not only that those who sack him have a monopoly on truth, but that the rest of us cannot make up our own minds about the value of Mr Hoddle's monstrous beliefs. It implies that we need protecting from his dreadful influence.

What is more, by sacking Mr Hoddle for insulting the disabled, his sackers have further insulted the disabled. By sacking him they have implied that the disabled need defending against the charge of being punished by God and that they cannot defend themselves. But they can defend themselves. They can defend themselves in one simple, robust and splendidly human way – they can burst out laughing.

Inadvertently Mr Hoddle may have done the world a favour. By talking such drivel he may have highlighted the lunacy of faith healing, New Age evangelism and all the other bunkum from tarot cards to palm reading that passes for thought, and in doing so he may have reduced by a jot the credulity of people. And if he has, I share Dave Collier's belief that a malt whisky should be named after him, and I will cheerfully raise a glass of it to toast his health.

The devil's abroad

Travel broadens the mind. For this reason I avoid it. Besides, I have dogs. It is hard to travel with dogs and impossible to put them in kennels. But then last weekend friends asked me to visit with dogs. The dogs could sleep in the house, they said. There was space for them to run. There were no sheep for miles. It sounded too good to be true, but I went.

It was too good to be true. There was a goat.

I cannot see the point of goats. Goats eat gorse, socks and plastic with equal pleasure. Truck batteries can run off a goat's digestive juices. Goats smell like goats. Their cheese smells like sewage. Goats butt, kick and look stupid.

In America, randy is a Christian name. Everywhere else, randy is a goat, for people since time began have linked goats with lechery. Lechery is sin, sin is the devil and the devil has goat hoofs, goat eyes, goat horns and a vacuous goat grin. It is said that once a day every goat visits the devil to have his beard combed. I believe it.

For obvious reasons, then, I have had little to do with goats. I have had even less to do with horses. Once, however, I had too much to do with both at the same time. It was all the fault of a rich girl called Zippy. She was called Zippy for reasons disappointingly innocent, but she made up for that innocence by having horses. Horses terrify me. They have teeth and nostrils and back legs. One afternoon Zippy asked if I had ever ridden a horse. I coughed modestly and murmured that I had. I was going on to say that I had been six at the time and the horse had been twenty-seven but before you could say terror we were out in the paddock and I was being helped onto a stallion called, if I remember rightly, Bowel-tightener. Bowel-tightener was huge but it accepted me onto its back with ominous calm. When I struggled finally into a sitting position, it still didn't move, nor even when I swivelled to face in the right direction.

'Say trot', said Zippy. I said 'Trot' and to my astonishment, we trotted. I felt like Mark Todd.

I don't know what Mark Todd is like at spotting goats. I'm quite good at it. I spotted the goat on the far side of the paddock almost immediately. Bowel-tightener took five seconds to spot the goat but made up for the delay by launching into an instant gallop goatward. I do not know if the horse was driven by affection or by hatred and at the time I didn't enquire. I was more concerned with screaming. Then the goat went behind a bush. 'What goat where?' said Bowel-tightener's tiny brain to its monstrous body, and the horse stopped. I chose that moment to effect a forward dismount double somersault with one and a half twists, degree of difficulty a week in bed with Lucozade.

So much then for my acquaintance with goats, until, that is, last weekend when I woke in a bed which I didn't recognise but for the two square metres of dogflesh stretched out over most of it. It was six in the morning. The dogs suggested we go exploring.

The little township was asleep, the air had an autumnal edge, the light was like shattered glass and I felt in dreadful danger of writing poetry. Until, that is, we turned into Goat Street.

It wasn't called Goat Street but it should have been, for on a steep and rugged slope beneath a house on poles, stood a ruminating pot-bellied billy. The dogs dived over the rim and down the slope. They wanted goat. The goat was tethered. One dog barked rampant at the goat's nose, the other at its heels. The goat lowered its head and surged but was brought up short by its tether. The dogs exulted. I whistled them, but might as well have whistled Jesus.

The goat surged again, uprooted its tether and charged the white dog who bounded across the hill, delighted with fright. I shouted. In Goat House a curtain opened and a sleepy accusing face appeared at the window. I waved cheerfully then launched myself into Goat Gulch. The three beasts thundered past me. I slithered down the slope, dived to tackle a dog, grabbed an armful of air and rolled deftly into a boulder. Applause. I looked up to see two women in nightgowns and a man in Paisley pyjamas standing on the deck. They were laughing.

I waved and shrugged to the crowd, as if to say sorry to wake you but you know how it is. One of the women shouted. I did not make out the words but I smiled back as if I did. The goat slammed into the back of my legs. I re-enacted my dismount routine. The boulder had not got any softer.

It wasn't until the man in pyjamas came down to retether the goat that I managed to secure the dogs. I drove home that afternoon. Travel is perilous. The devil is abroad. I shall keep to a narrow mind.

Words on books

First, the good news: Lyttelton has a new library. Instead of an old cold building we now have something that is warm and modern. Although the building has been painted the colour of fresh lung tissue, its atmosphere is inviting, the carpet is scattered with cushions for children to lie on and the whole of Lyttelton rejoices. Apart, that is, from the people who did not want money spent on a library. They wanted it spent on sewerage.

I can think of nicer things than a library – things I like to eat, drink or nuzzle – but I can think of nothing more civilised than a library. Libraries contain books, books contain language, and as I have said before and shall no doubt say again, language is what distinguishes us from the beasts of the field and the fans of the sewerage system.

As people we stand on the shoulders of the dead. What the dead have thought and felt lives on in books. Hitler burnt books. Mao burnt books. Stalin burnt books. If you burn books it is a short and inevitable step to burning people, a step which Hitler, Mao and Stalin found they had to take. And having taken it they found they had to take it again and again and again and the burning books and people multiplied and the smoke so filled the nostrils of those who had yet to burn that it became only a matter of time before Hitler, Mao and Stalin fell. Evil can take a long time to fall. Indeed, all of these tyrants managed to die in office, but by then they had forfeited their humanity, their lives rang hollow, and those who inherited their palaces found that they were built on sand. Those palaces soon fell, as they were bound to do. Once again the old story is confirmed that he who burns books, lights his own funeral pyre.

The Greeks invented libraries, of course, just as they invented the patterns of Western thought. The Greek library in Alexandria held perhaps half a million handwritten volumes.

In 642, Caliph Omar and his Muslim army sacked Alexandria and burnt the books. The Western world took 500 years to recover. One of my more fervent wishes is that deep in the sewers of hell Caliph Omar lies on a bed of razor blades, and that a private devil reads to him night and day from the memoirs of Jim Bolger.

Now for the bad news. In today's paper I read about New Zealand's National Library, and here, in full, is what I read.

'The National Library will shed sixty jobs in restructuring. Library staff in Wellington and service centres around the country are being given details of the strategic plan, spokeswoman Belinda Howard said. The new structure would mean changes in the library's core business.'

I am sure that Belinda Howard is kind to children and puppies, but her words are bad. She has entered the murk of consultancy-speak, where what you say is not what you mean, where what you say is indeed designed to conceal what you mean, even perhaps from the speaker, because the truth isn't nice.

Ms Howard tells us that the library will shed jobs. 'Shed' is the wrong verb. Snakes shed dead skin; trees shed dead leaves. Shedding leaves or skin is a natural process, but sacking librarians is a conscious decision. And the librarians who will be sacked are flesh and blood. Ms Howard's words lie.

According to Ms Howard, the library will not shrink. Instead it will 'restructure'. Restructuring always means sacking people. I am only surprised that Ms Howard did not add that they were streamlining their operations in response to market forces.

The National Library does not run branch libraries any more. It runs service centres. Service centres are such pale things that one doesn't mind seeing them laid waste. Who can weep for a service centre? And behind it all lurks a strategic plan. One might have guessed.

To top it off, the library is to change its 'core business'. The National Library is not, of course, a business, but if it were, its job would be to preserve the intellectual harvest of this nation. Ms

Howard suggests that this will now change.

It is possible that the National Library is changing for the better, but I doubt it. I doubt it because of the words used. Miss Howard uses the euphemistic jargon of the business world. Such language has no place in a library, least of all in the National Library which is our treasure house of words.

I cannot tell you how the weasel words managed to burrow into that treasure house, but I can tell you what that noise is beneath your feet. It is Caliph Omar in the sewers of hell. And he is laughing.

Neerg fingers

How excellent to see garden centres being prosecuted for trading over Easter when you and I were busy with God. I should like to see garden centres prosecuted far more often on any pretext whatsoever. They need spraying with a sort of legal Roundup till the garden centre owners with their grubby fingernails and unthinkable underwear finally give up altogether and close down for the greater good of mankind.

I read somewhere – no, it doesn't matter where; frankly it wasn't the sort of publication that I care to be known to have read – that gardening is the preferred leisure activity of about 98% of the population. Anyone who has a 'preferred leisure activity' at all, or indeed anyone who can read the words 'preferred leisure activity' without gagging, is quite beyond redemption and should be condemned to watch 5.30 with Jude until their kidneys implode. Anyway, if the statistics are even remotely accurate then all hope is lost and our only salvation is anthrax in the water supply.

Yes, yes, I know, you don't have to tell me, I just haven't got the patience or the love of nature to garden. I'm full of angst and arrogance and out of sync with chlorophyll. I simply envy the green-fingered ones.

Well, let me tell you something. I may not be Capability Brown, but I'm as much in touch with nature as the next man. Barely a week goes by without me winding the car window down to get a good deep sniff of the stuff.

On the gardening charge I will confess to having the opposite of green fingers – neerg fingers I suppose – but I have learnt to wear my neerginess with pride.

When we neergs plant things they die. One minute they're sitting up all cheerful and bushy in their little plastic nappies on the wet sawdust at the garden centre, the next they're in my garden and instantly horizontal and fermenting the sort of gases that puncture ozone. I used to find it depressing and expensive. Now I don't care. If ever the urge to do a spot of gardening wells up these days I just go out and ram a few twenty-dollar bills into the soil. They're the right colour and it saves on petrol and they don't need watering.

All garden centres – why 'centres' anyway? – should be prosecuted, but there should also be a special prosecutor, a sort of NZ Torquemada, appointed to hunt down and torture the owners of garden centres that sell native plants. Native plants are mind-murderingly drab. They are all called Pittosporum banksii and they come in green or green. A native plant's idea of flowering is to put out three millimetres of pale-green petal beneath a leaf for two days a decade. Note how natives are always planted round shoddy new housing and on the malarial rims of industrial eyesores. They are economy vegetation serving only to mask woven wire fences and oil-soaked, crap-strewn, guard-dog-guarded repositories for lumps of dead engine.

And oh the prejudice of gardeners. They discriminate between plants on utterly spurious grounds. I once heard a large woman define a weed as anything that didn't need her help to grow. That's horticultural apartheid.

What's more, it confirms my suspicion that all gardeners are closet self-flagellants. If dandelions were hard to grow gardeners would salivate over their dense golden beauty and the ineffable tuftiness of their fruiting pods. But they aren't hard to grow so gardeners get down on their knees with their little dibbers and their dinky little bottles of paraquat and they seek out the innocent little darlings and they kill them.

Neergs don't. We like dandelions. I've now got a 500 square metre dandelion and money farm. It will be open to the public for tours, starting next Easter.

The good reverend

The Reverend Graham Capill and I have three things in common. We both have, as far as I am aware, the regulation number of limbs, and we are both partial to oxygen, though I prefer mine laced with a few hundred carcinogens. Our third point of similarity is that neither of us has read *Dare, Truth or Promise* by Paula Boock, the recent winner of the supreme prize and the senior fiction category of the NZ Post Children's Book of the Year Contest.

At that point I am afraid the likeness peters out.

It was Sydney Smith who said, 'I never read a book before reviewing it, it prejudices a man so.' Clearly the Rev. S. Smith and the Rev. G. Capill have much in common, except that the Rev. S. Smith was funny.

The Rev. G. Capill has rather gone to town on the book he hasn't read, and in particular on its being chosen as a prize winner. He has described the judges' acclaim of the book he hasn't read as 'unbelievably warped'. The book he hasn't read is 'inherently unsuitable' for the teenage audience at which it is aimed, because of its 'warped moral values'.

Well, that's strong talk, Rev, and, if I might suggest, rather unwise talk. Teenagers tend to be fond of warped moral values. I fear that the reverend's hasty words might cause a stampede to the school library.

And what will our vulnerable teenagers find when they batter down the doors and ransack the shelves in search of *Dare, Truth or Promise*? An illustrated history of torture? Your hundred best stills from snuff videos? Thirty-six ways to make a reliable bomb?

No, apparently – for remember that I have not read the book either – they will find a tale of the lesbian love of two teenagers, a tale written with, one can only presume, such economy, sensitivity and truth to life that a panel of literary people judged it the best book of the hundreds put before them.

So why is the good reverend so upset? Well, the most obvious reason, for it drips from his words like pus, is that he thinks lesbians are 'warped'. He is entitled to hold that opinion, although it does not seem to me to sit prettily with Christ's injunction to love one's neighbour, which the Rev. G. Capill, as leader of a Christian party, must surely have heard of. I would not wish to be Reverend Capill's neighbour and a lesbian – though I hasten to reassure readers that I am in little danger of being either.

Secondly, the reverend's words show a touching faith in the power of literature. Implicit in his words is the belief that if one reads about lesbianism one is more likely to become lesbian. If he did not believe that, he would be fulminating against this book simply because it described something he did not like.

Well, I don't like motor racing, indeed I find it morally warped, but if I plunged slavering into Whitcoulls and set about ripping up *Fifty Years of Formula One* I think I would be due for the straitjacket.

So, assuming the Rev. G. Capill is not mad – a large assumption, I admit, but let us make it – it must be his view that this book will drive the girls of New Zealand into each other's arms to do whatever it is that lesbians do.

Well, I recently read a book on cannibalism and I can safely say that it has not increased one jot my desire to bone, joint and roast the Rev. G. Capill and tuck into his drumsticks. Nor would books on crochet, croquet or terrorism induce me to indulge in any of these three equally scary activities.

But, the reverend will no doubt say, Joe Bennett is not an impressionable teenager. He is a gentleman of mature years, intellectual eminence, stately bearing and a mind as unimpressionable as granite. Gee, thank you, Graham, that's uncommonly kind. I think very highly of you too. But I am afraid I cannot quite accept your argument.

The only way in which a book, film, play or painting is going to influence my behaviour is if it releases in me something which was already there. The same is true for pensioners, priests and, yes, teenagers. The only girls who might be encouraged by *Dare, Truth or Promise* to flirt with lesbianism, are those with some predisposition to do so. I do not think it is a bad thing if they do so flirt. I am sure the Rev. G. Capill thinks it is.

And now it is time to stop pussyfooting, so to speak.

How dare he? I mean, how dare he? Has he no idea what he is doing? Has he no idea of the damage caused by self-repression? Has he no idea of the number of teenagers in this country who are tortured by feelings they dare not explore or express? Has he no idea of the self-hatred, the secrecy, the paranoia that such attitudes as his have bred over the years? Has he no sense of the damage wreaked by his own smug, hideous, bull-necked prejudice?

I feel better for that. Just as several teenage girls will feel better for having read *Dare, Truth or Promise*. They will feel that they are not alone, that it is okay to be who they are.

And for the others who read it, the vast majority who are not so affected, the novel might just enlighten them and might just help produce a generation of more tolerant people. People, Reverend Capill, who love their neighbours.

Lies

There we were, dining tête-à-tête in a candle-lit restaurant off Manchester Street and things were a bit sticky. She had accused me of, not to put too fine a point on it, lying to her.

I said there were lies everywhere and drew her attention to the oxtail soup. I asked her why, if oxtails were so good, had I never knowingly eaten any other parts of an ox? I said I didn't see the country infested by docked oxen. The answer, of course, is that oxtails are actually cow tails but cow tail soup sounds a bit too nasty because we've all seen cow tails swishing expressively in paddocks, and being, how shall we say, just a little besmeared, so oxtail soup's a lie. Indeed it's such a good lie that butchers fool people with it. 'So you see,' I said with the merest hint of triumph, 'lies are everywhere,' and I called for another bowl of oxtail just to celebrate the great human skill of lying.

Where would we be without lies? There'd be no television news or pop songs or advertisements or any of the things that make life worth living. I went to Czechoslovakia years ago before it became two places that nobody's heard of, back in the good old days when Moscow's merry fist slammed down on any Vladimir who even thought of putting a foot out of line, and Czechoslovakia in those days was not only unspellable but it was also seriously grim. It was all grey concrete and grey snow and bad beer and worse sausages, and it took me a while to work out what was wrong and what was wrong was it lacked lies. There wasn't an ad to be seen, not a single poster telling you that if you used deodorant you'd have to hire a Dobermann to fight the women off, or if you went to Vanuatu everybody would smile at you – not that Czechs could go to Vanuatu because passports were as rare as happiness – and so the poor old downtrodden Czechs just muttered their way around dirty streets eating cabbage, knowing there was no prospect of anything but cabbage tomorrow and so looking truth in the eye and being, in consequence, very sad indeed. What they needed was a sprinkling of lies. 'And of course, darling,' I said to her, 'the irony of the whole thing…'

'The what?' she said.

'The irony, darling, irony,' but she hadn't heard of it so I gave up.

'My simple point is, sweetie,' I said, 'that lying is fun and dangerous and human and creative and necessary for the maintenance of sanity. Animals can't do it and we can and there's an end to it. And there's little joy to be got from truth,' I said. 'I mean truth's one of two things: it's either nasty or it's boring or it's false.'

She said that was three things but I swept on.

'First,' I said, 'nasty truth, like we're all going to die, or being young ought to be good but we spend most of it being miserable, or being old ought to be nasty and is, so we spend it wishing we were young, or time is cruel and all the other stuff of poetry. That's nasty truth,' I said, 'and then there's boring truth which is the grisly details of reality, all the sordid little worries about money and sex, and unsatisfactory washing machines and watching Coronation Street and fiddling the income tax and yearning for outdoor furniture from The Warehouse. That's the boring truth,' I said, 'and then there's the false truth.'

'False truth?' she said.

'False truth,' I said, 'like American how-to-become-rich books, or opinion polls or I love you.'

'You do?' she said.

'I do,' I said.

I believe

It is a relief to know that the Western world is in good hands. Last week the President of the United States retired to Martha's Vineyard to rebuild his marriage. As any counsellor will tell you, the only way for a wayward husband to make it up to his wife is to play golf with billionaires. So there was Mr Clinton, hacking his way through the rough of Hillary's displeasure, when all of a sudden duty called.

You and I would have told duty to go and wait with a gin in the clubhouse, but neither you nor I are President of the United States. In a fairer world, of course, we would be, but for now the job has gone to the jogger with the chubby legs.

Anyway, last Friday, old Martha was merrily trampling out the vintage when a telegram from the Pentagon comes knocking at the vineyard door. Mr Clinton scans the telegram, drops his three-iron and, with a cry of 'My country needs me' jumps onto the first available intern. Security hauls him off and flies him to Washington.

Mr Clinton has a special voice which he pulls out for the big occasions. He used it to tell us that he hadn't had sex with Monica Lewinsky. He also used it to tell us that he had had sex with Monica Lewinsky. Last week he used it to tell us that America has identified and deployed its full military might against global enemy number one, that threat to life, liberty and the American way, Something Bin Something.

We learnt that Mr Bin Something comes from Saudi Arabia and is very rich. Nevertheless he chooses to live in a tent in Afghanistan. This may be because when it comes to terrorism, Afghans take the biscuit, but more likely it is because it makes him into the perfect bogeyman.

CIA intelligence – anyone for oxymoron? – has proved beyond

doubt that Mr Bin Something is a terrorist. For a start, they have pointed out that Mr Bin Something wears cloth on his head. This means he's an Arab and probably a relative of Yasser Arafat.

Secondly he lives in a place which sounds really suspicious.

Thirdly, he looks a bit like a Klingon.

Faced with this proof that Mr Bin Something masterminded the embassy bombings, the World Trade Centre bombing, the Lockerbie plane crash, the Californian earthquake and the AIDS epidemic, it was clear that the United States of America had to act. Furthermore it was vital to act last Friday for a multitude of reasons which the CIA have listed and which I will quote in full:

1. The President had just admitted having sex with Monica Lewinsky.

So President Clinton ordered his navy to fire missiles onto the sovereign territory of other countries. There used to be a word for this robust style of diplomacy. That word was war.

After World War Two the world created the United Nations to stop war. It has done an excellent job except when countries have decided to go to war. Also, because it has lots more weapons than anyone else and it owes lots of money to the United Nations, America has always felt free to invade anyone it likes whenever it likes.

So the missiles flew and the One Network News team's coverage treated us to exciting pictures of simulated missiles cruising over simulated bits of Africa and the Middle East. In deepest Sudan they blew up an aspirin factory. As the aspirins rained from the sky every Sudanese with a headache rejoiced, apart, that is, from the Sudanese who were in the factory. Their headaches took a turn for the worse.

The CIA had two excellent reasons to bomb the factory:

1. It had been manufacturing nerve gas.
2. The President had just admitted having sex with Monica Lewinsky.

The Sudanese have protested to the United Nations. That will do them a lot of good. What they haven't done is to express any worry about the deadly chemicals which have presumably been showered over Khartoum. I find this surprising.

Meanwhile America approves of the bombing. Even though Mr Clinton spent last week owning up to lies, eighty per cent of Americans have apparently believed his story about Mr Bin Something and the aspirin factory.

Mr Bin Something will soon have served his purpose whereupon he will fade quietly away and leave not a wrack behind. A year from now his name will mean nothing.

Meanwhile, however, Madeleine Albright has warned the American people to be vigilant. Retaliation could come at any moment. I will be a little less than surprised if that moment coincides with the publication of a report by a certain Mr Starr.

Forget *Wag the Dog*. Has anyone here read *1984*?

Knickers

Mr William Geddie's twentieth century differed from mine. As you may know, Mr William Geddie M.A. edited *The Chambers Twentieth Century Dictionary* and it was to him that I turned last week to look up the word 'knickers'. You don't need to know why. Anyway, Mr Geddie informed me that knickerbockers were women's undergarments gathered at the knee, but of knickers he said nothing at all.

Under 'knicker' he told me to go to 'nicker'. I went, and found that a nicker is a water monster. It is also a Scottish laugh and a round seed used for playing marbles, all of which are great fun but awkward under a skirt. In Mr Geddie's twentieth century knickers didn't exist.

But I don't know what else to call women's undergarments. Bloomers are a joke, undies infantile, pants trousers, underpants male and panties twee.

Lingerie sings of silken self-indulgence, but no one can pronounce it except the French and, as every schoolboy knows, Frenchwomen don't wear knickers.

The most signal truth about knickers is that women need to own about a hundred pairs, i.e. one for every pair of shoes. Of the women I have known well, both had a drawer so crammed with knickers that when you hauled it open the things sprang at you.

For years we men have watched the female fascination with underwear with baffled curiosity. But now the tables are turning, for of late the manufacturers of underwear have swung the ruthless spotlight of their advertising onto men.

Today as I drove to work I was confronted by a man recumbent on a billboard. His hair was long, his smile laconic, body bronzed and muscles taut. Amidships he sported a pair of lime-green underpants. They were called Hunks. The Hunks harboured a squid.

In Mr Geddie's day men's underpants went unconsidered except for the weekly change of yellowing Y-fronts. This change was like the peeling of skin. But now in every menswear shop there stands a rack of brand-name underwear. Each is advertised by the mandatory youth with a flopping fringe and the figure of a Greek discus thrower.

And the advertising works. Having checked that there is no one we know at the checkout, we buy our Hunks, Chunks or Woppers and we bear them home like contraband. In the privacy of the bedroom we cram ourselves into them and pose before the mirror in the manner of bodybuilders.

What we seek is youth. What we see is sagging dugs and missing muscles. We shake what is left of our hair. The dandruff falls like a Christmas paperweight and weary with disillusion we cram the underpants into the back of a drawer like a letter from abroad that we will never answer.

For as the commercial world turns its attention increasingly to men, exhorting us to groom ourselves, to spray ourselves, to care how we appear, we of the Play-Doh bellies are learning at last how women have felt all these years; we are learning the humiliation of imperfection.

I think, on balance, I prefer Mr Geddie's twentieth century to my own.

A-gley

'The best laid schemes o' mice an' men,' said Robbie Burns, 'gang aft a-gley,' a truism which has reminded countless generations of the folly of trying to understand the Scots.

I was reminded of the expression the other day by Margaret. 'You have to go to Auckland,' Margaret had said, 'for an interview.'

My heart swelled like a cabbage.

'Auckland,' I exclaimed, 'that cosmopolitan metropolis where life travels at breakneck speed and whose streets are paved with the corpses of those who couldn't keep up.'

Margaret got caught up in my excitement.

'Yes,' she said.

'Hot diggety dawg,' I said.

Suppressing her joy behind a frosty brow, Margaret handed me my travel plans. I danced a jig of joy which involved the adroit head-butting of a fluorescent tube.

'Leave it,' said Margaret, 'I'll clean it up. Remember the interview is early in the morning. It's important. Stay off the booze and don't be late.'

'Never fear,' I exclaimed.

It was then that Margaret quoted Robbie Burns, whereupon I chuckled a nonchalant chuckle, waved a nonchalant wave and headed home to lay plans.

I arranged to stay with Gareth in a bijou apartmentette in Remuera where I arrived in the late afternoon. Gareth was out, so I headed into Remmers to test the waters. By chance I met Gareth in the street, and he urged me to share a water with him.

'No no,' I exclaimed, 'call me Goody Two Shoes but I have to be up early in the morning, perky as a perky thing.'

'Heineken?' asked Gareth.

'Thank you,' I said, and we fell to watching the sea of tanned bodies and black dresses that washed along Remuera Road like a costly tide. The women were well dressed too, but soon it was time for me to leave for dinner with a former colleague whose life has taken her from the swamps of Christchurch to the plateau of Parnell.

'I'll not be late back,' I told Gareth.

'The key's on the window sill,' he said.

Friday night in Parnell and the recession was in full swing. Gloomy patrons spilled onto the pavement from every bar and restaurant, weeping noisily into their Bollinger. After a wait of barely an hour we secured a table in a Italian joint where I was all abstemiousness. Having wrung the dregs from bottle three, I kissed my former colleague goodbye smack on midnight, poured myself into a taxi and returned to Remmers.

The key was on the window sill, and a bed had been laid out on the living room floor, along with an alarm clock and a thoughtful little packet of aspirins. The window looked out over a garden where the neighbour was winding up an alfresco dinner party by playing the accordion. It was unreasonable behaviour and I opened the window to remonstrate.

'Oi,' I remonstrated, 'may I join you?'

The neighbour, it transpired, lived in one of those freaky time zones. Though I stayed less than an hour it was five o'clock when I got in. When I say 'got in' I mean that I reached the door at five. The window sill was bare. Roused by my merry knocking Gareth was all smiles. He was also all smiles a little while later when he came into the living room and invited me to turn the alarm off.

I glanced at the clock, took a leisurely ten-second shower, a handful of aspirins and a spoonful of peanut butter, and sprinted for a taxi. Fifteen minutes later, as I awaited the interview, I decided that the peanut butter had been an error of judgement.

At Christchurch airport Margaret asked me how the interview had gone. I groped for the apt words but they eluded me, just as, I dimly remembered, they had in the interview. But then I struck gold.

'A-gley,' I said, 'it ganged a-gley.'

Margaret managed to conceal her mirth behind a frosty silence.

Angels and warthogs

Pablo Picasso could draw like an angel. I have seen film of Picasso drawing a bull on a guitar. He captured the essence of bull in a single line.

His was a glorious gift, for to make art is to reach for something beyond ourselves. It is to snatch at eternity. It is what makes us human.

But for some reason Picasso the angel spent most of his life drawing like a warthog. Of course Picasso was free to do as he wished with his talent, but I find it hard to forgive him his legacy. More than any other painter, Picasso the warthog must take the blame for the tosh that infests most modern art galleries, tosh produced by painters who are long on warthog but short on angel. When I start my aesthetic revolution, and the time is drawing near, these artists will be the first against the wall.

In his private life Picasso was neither warthog nor angel. He was a lusty soul who attracted a stream of wives and mistresses. Quite why artists attract women I don't know. Perhaps the women sniff eternity. Or good sex. Or both.

Anyway, with the gallantry typical of the Spanish caballero, Picasso painted his womenfolk. In homage to their charms he painted portraits which made them look like geometry with eyes. The eyes fell in strange places. Most of the women left soon after they were painted.

One of these women has just died and a London auction house has sold her collection of Picasso stuff. There were many paintings. There were also doodles and other Picasso trivia. The auction grossed $60m. Among the buyers, one lucky bidder parted with only a few hundred dollars and scuttled into the night clutching to his or her breast a paper napkin torn by the hand of the master himself into the shape of what may or may not be a ferret.

What I want to ask is why. Why did someone pay money for a napkin that had been clumsily torn by a drunken Spaniard for his lover sixty years ago.

On one level the answer is obvious – the man who tore the napkin was Picasso. On another level it is less obvious. A torn napkin is a torn napkin. That it was torn by Picasso does not make it art. It doesn't even make it well torn.

Imagine that someone managed to prove that the napkin had come from McDonald's and had been torn by one of those scrofulous youths who ask you if you want fries even though you didn't ask for fries. The napkin's value would drain instantly to zilch.

So, the napkin's value lies purely in its association with Picasso. This reminds me of nothing so much as the medieval world, when there was big money in religious relics. Churches around Europe held enough pieces of the true cross to build an ark. They supplemented these with such splendid trophies as the tibia of Mary Magdalene or, honestly, the Relic of the Holy Circumcision. There were three of these.

Today we laugh at such mummery. But every purchase of a miniskirt worn by Ginger Spice, a microphone licked by Hendrix, or a napkin torn by Picasso shows the same instinct at work in a secular age. It is a vain snatch at eternity by association. And it doesn't work.

Could do better

One purpose of a school report is to tell the parents how their child is doing at school. An equally important purpose is to make the teacher look good.

If a child performs poorly parents tend to blame the teacher. Teachers don't like to be blamed so they mask the problem with words. 'Anthony is easily distracted,' means he doesn't do any work. 'Anthony's attention span could be improved,' means he doesn't do any work. 'Anthony has organisational problems,' means he doesn't bring any books.

My own school reports of thirty years ago were simple affairs. I still have one from the fourth form. Under each subject there's a percentage figure and a comment. I was a swot. Physics says 'good'. Latin says 'chatterbox'. All the others say 'sound progress'. The headmaster, a man of flair, put the incisive personal touch to the report by writing the only complete sentence. 'Bennett is making sound progress,' he wrote.

Reports like these came on a single sheet of paper. Teachers like these reports because they can see what everyone else has written. If six other teachers write that Blank is keen and diligent, it does not pay to write that Blank farts and fights. Blank's wind and wounds become the teacher's fault.

Many school reports these days are written, however, on separate sheets which are then collated into a booklet. These present the teacher with two problems. The first is that they provide too much space to fill. The second is that the teachers are writing in isolation.

Many teachers resort to the noble arts of bombast and euphemism. Modern educational jargon comes in handy here, the sort of jargon that NZQA produces by the ream and which makes as much sense as the Roswell incident. With practice a teacher can learn to spout mounds of the stuff. 'This term we have focused on listening skills. Jemima has learned to process aural information from a range of authentic contexts and has gained a satisfactory grasp of the concepts involved.'

The computer helps here. Once a teacher has created a magnificent sentence like this he can cut and paste it onto every report at the touch of a key.

On several occasions in my teaching career I have seen phantom reports. These are reports for pupils who have long since left the school but somehow remained in the records. Administration has churned out a blank report for the child and teachers have filled it in. Most of the teachers report that the non-existent student, though quiet in class, has worked steadily. Once, however, a magnificently incompetent geography teacher in Canada, made a point of praising the lively contribution to class discussion made by a boy who had died in the holidays.

In almost twenty years of teaching I have written about 10,000 reports. I am proud of two of them. One said simply, 'Yes'. The headmaster sent it back to me.

The other occurred in the days of single-page reports. It did not pay to make an error on such a report because it meant that every teacher had to rewrite his comment. This particular report was for a boy called James. Someone distracted me as I went to write. In consequence I began my report, 'David…' It was the end of term and half the teachers had already gone home. I couldn't possibly force a rewrite.

'David eventually slew Goliath,' I wrote, 'and James might finally master spelling.' The comment bore no relation to James' performance, but that, of course, didn't matter at all. It was a splendid report.

Gloat-free zone

William Jefferson Clinton – and don't you just love the Jefferson – has been acquitted of charges of perjury and obstruction of justice. According to Reuter, people around the world are relieved that the trial is over and Washington can return to more important matters. Clearly there are many things more important than lying under oath and tampering with court proceedings when holding the highest office in the land.

Mr Clinton's people have declared the White House a gloat-free zone, a phrase which echoes the no-fly zone in Iraq. The no-fly zone exists because Saddam Hussein wants to fly in it. Similarly the gloat-free zone exists because Mr Clinton's people want to gloat.

If the White House felt no urge to gloat they would not have thought to mention gloating. And if they had felt the urge to gloat but genuinely known that they had nothing to gloat about, they would have said, 'We shall try not to gloat.'

But the twisters of opinion do not speak so directly because they do not tell the truth. They chose a phrase that echoes military tactics because they are engaged in a battle for public goodwill. They understand emotion only as something to manipulate to gain a political end, and the only political end they can see is the oldest of them all, the maintenance of power.

But I bet they have gloated. In a secure room at the back of the White House they will have drawn the curtains, cracked a crate of champagne and danced on the eighteenth-century furniture, before emerging to meet the cameras with faces as long as Sunday afternoon.

A sentence in the Reuter report tells us that 'Mr Clinton and his aides had an intense behind-the-scenes debate over his reaction to the Senate vote'. Those few words expose the fallacy at the heart of this business.

I do not for one moment doubt that they did debate his reaction, but by doing so they condemn themselves, because one cannot debate how someone reacts. Reaction is involuntary. What they debated was not how Mr Clinton reacted, but how he should appear to react. They were creating an act, a lie to add to the wad of lies that Mr Clinton has already told and which he has just been acquitted of telling.

The spontaneous reaction that the collected aides, advisers, cronies, leeches, crawlers, spin doctors, coat-tail hangers and other Harvard graduates eventually chose for Mr Clinton to exhibit to the world was as predictable as a conveyor belt. It was also a reaction that Mr Clinton does well. He lowers his voice, keeps his head very still, looks deep into the heart of his friend the television camera, and utters platitudes.

The language Mr Clinton uses means nothing. It resembles the little hammer that doctors use to tap kneecaps. Just as doctors are seeking to excite a nerve over which we have no control, so Mr Clinton is seeking to arouse an emotional response at a level below conscious thought.

He first taps the patriotic nerve by referring in every other sentence to 250 million heterogeneous individuals as 'the American people'. He then goes on to tap the religious nerve by numerous references to God.

His sentences swell with empty rhetoric. 'Now I ask all Americans, and I hope all Americans, here in Washington and throughout our land, will rededicate ourselves to the work of serving our nation and building our future together.' The flattering implication, of course, is that Americans have already dedicated themselves with such selfless nobility. The truth is that they haven't and they won't. But it sounds good.

The whole of the speech amounted to 'business as usual, folks. I've still got my job.'

At the end of the speech, a reporter who may or may not have been a plant, asked Mr Clinton if he could forgive his enemies.

'I believe,' said Mr Clinton, 'any person who asks for forgiveness has to be prepared to give it.' Here we have the simple, heart-warming, bedrock morality of Grandpa Walton. One would need a heart of granite to condemn such a man.

Mr Clinton is not the first president of the United States to be a philanderer, nor the first to tell fibs. But his extraordinary perform-ance over recent months has been exactly that, a performance, an act of expedience cloaked in the language of sincerity. From his use of spiritual advisers to his recent magnanimity he has attempted to hijack our better feelings in order to serve his own ends. The two truths we can draw from this are not new truths, but they are crucial truths – that power can intoxicate people and that language can con people.

We will hold an election here this year. We would do well to remember these truths. But we won't.

God bless America.

From here to prostate

I was pretending to read a plastic picture card telling me how to jump out of the plane, but surreptitiously I was scanning the passengers coming down the aisle for the one who would sit next to me. I have a gift for attracting the seriously religious and mothers with psychotic infants. Somehow you always know who's going to sit beside you the moment you see them. Perhaps it's the dangling saliva.

She had to squeeze past me to get to the window seat. Aeroplane friendships always begin with your eyes about eight inches from the other's crotch, the sort of position it can take a normal friendship a good month to attain, if ever. Such instant proximity can break the ice, of course. It can also thicken it.

'These seats are made for anorexics,' she said. I could detect no hint of religion in the sentence, and if there was a psychotic infant then she had stowed it in the overhead locker, which was just fine by me. On Bennett Airlines, all children travel as freight.

Anyway, as opening comments go this one seemed to go pretty well. I decided to risk a flight's-worth of evangelism by an expansive gesture of friendship. I flicked an eyebrow and expelled a little air through one nostril. It's one of my more effective come-ons.

Two minutes later I had tucked the picture card back in that nifty little seat pocket and was ignoring the safety pantomime starring a bored stewardess and an implausible oxygen mask that is attached to nothing but which one is supposed to tug. There's no point in watching it. Just as I know that I like Guinness, have never grown up and can't stop smoking, so I know with equal certainty that in the event of an air accident I would exhibit without hesitation my talent for panic.

But this was not why I was ignoring the panto on this occasion.

Rather my attention was held elsewhere, for beside me, I had discovered, was sitting a creature whom I had never thought about before but whom, if I had ever got round to thinking about her, I would have presumed not to exist.

Barbara, for that was her name – well, actually it wasn't; I can't quite remember her name but I think it had the same number of syllables – lived in Southland, which of course is nothing remarkable – several people have been doing it for years and don't seem much the worse for the experience – but the extraordinary thing is that Barbara, or rather 'Barbara', made her living down there where the nights are long and the grass longer, by selling, wait for it, vitamins.

I think I had better repeat that, without any of those interruptions which seem to be creeping into the sentences today – not that I mind them, of course, in fact I think they add a ring of authenticity, the stamp of a mind in action, don't you think? Anyway, Barbara, or rather 'Barbara', (you're with me? good) sold vitamins, which she pronounced vi-tamins whereas I was brought up to say vit-amins, not that it makes much difference I suppose, in Southland. Is that clearer now? Have you latched on to the full import of that statement?

Now, I'm no Ranulph Fiennes, but I have been to Southland. Last year. January. High summer. Gore. Sunday afternoon. It was raining. Hard.

The main street of Gore was wide and wet – and empty but for two elderly men on stationary old-fashioned bicycles about ten feet apart outside the Four Square Superstore which was, astonishingly, closed. Both elderly men were wearing brown overcoats and cycle clips. Neither elderly man was looking at the other elderly man. Both elderly men were using battered vegetable knives to slash at their wrists.

All of the above is true apart from the bit about the vegetable knives. They may have been chisels. It was hard to tell at that distance and unfortunately the photos didn't come out. I needed a flash.

Anyway, that's all I know of Southland. So when 'Barbara' said she sold vi-tamins down there I thought of the two elderly men and I thought ah-ha and I said, eloquently, 'Oh.'

And as if that wasn't enough I added, 'So, how's business?'

'Booming,' said 'Barbara'.

I have never been one to fear repetition. If the word is right, use it as many times as you like. So I said, 'Oh' again.

'Barbara' looked me up and down. I could hardly begrudge her this look given my earlier intimacy with her crotch. She took in my thinning hair, and the other one that isn't thinning quite so badly. She took in my hammer toes. 'You need zinc,' she said.

We then had a witty little interchange about zinc. It went like this:

'Zinc?'

'Zinc.'

'Zinc?'

'Zinc.'

'Oh.'

Already half convinced I asked her why I needed zinc. 'Barbara' insisted that all men need zinc. It fixes everything.

'Everything?'

'From here to prostate.'

I immediately knew that I had got from this trip, if nothing else, the ideal title for every man's autobiography. I told her so.

'No,' said 'Barbara', 'from HAIR to prostate.'

'Oh,' I said, 'well, that's not bad either.'

She laughed. I laughed. We laughed all the way to Auckland. The flight took about ten minutes. She was a charming woman. But then she would have to be to sell vitamins in Gore.

Not that I'm a convert to vitamins, you understand. I will admit to having had, since my return, a nibble or two at a galvanised hinge on the laundry door, but that's only because there's nothing to lose. Soon hair will be a memory and the prostate prostrate. And then you jump out of the plane.

Baking nuts

There comes a time on a Sunday when the body craves something more substantial than aspirins. And it was at just this time last Sunday that I read an article about baking biscuits.

Grandmothers bake biscuits; I don't. I have never filled my tins.

But the article featured a recipe for ginger nuts. I love ginger nuts. Bite into a dry one and it's an even money bet whether tooth or biscuit will break first. Dunk a ginger nut in coffee, however, and it becomes a delicious confection which is easily spooned from the bottom of the cup. I read the recipe, I salivated and I decided I would bake.

Having ransacked the larder for ingredients, I rang a woman who knows. She told me that no, I couldn't really do without eggs or ground ginger. Nor could I substitute noodles for flour or beer for golden syrup.

I had to have baking soda too, apparently, but she reassured me that even if I never baked another biscuit my baking soda would not go to waste. I could clean the bath with it.

The woman who knows doesn't know my bath. Anything that could clean that bath has no business in biscuits. It would be more at home in a warhead.

My trip to the supermarket cost me a smidgen under fifteen dollars. I calculated that my home baking would power into profit after 500 biscuits.

In measuring 100 grams of butter the bathroom scales proved unsatisfactory, but all great cooks are innovators. On the 27th of July 1975 I took six wickets for forty-seven against Eastbourne, and was presented with the ball. It has travelled round the world with me.

A cricket ball weighs five and a half ounces. I tickled the calculator and found I needed two-thirds of a cricket ball of butter, one and a half cricket balls of sugar and one and three-quarters of flour.

After that it was a simple matter of placing the cricket ball in a bowl in the right hand and ingredients in a bowl in the left hand and seeing which way I leant.

I had to cream the sugar and butter. I presumed that cream meant beat. Creaming proved an efficient method of bending forks.

After five minutes creaming I had whipped up an arm full of lactic acid and the dogs had whipped up an enthusiasm for airborne lumps of sugared butter.

Add one tbsp of golden syrup. Golden syrup is not divisible into tbsps. It is not divisible into anything. However high you lift your tbsp it remains linked to the golden syrup tin by a rope of sagging sweetness. In the end the dogs solved the rope problem.

Sifting one and three-quarter cricket balls of flour from a height proved to be fun. Some of the flour landed in the bowl. Rather more landed on my black dog. When she sneezed she looked like the inside of a Christmas paperweight.

Creaming time again, then a pause to revive the creaming arm and straighten the creaming fork, before rolling the sludge into twenty-four golf balls and laying them on the baking tray I hadn't got. Improvising with tinfoil was genius, but transferring the foil to the oven proved costly. Balls roll. The dogs got seven of them raw.

Then all I had to do was turn the light on in the oven, pull up a chair and watch my balls become nuts. They sweated a little, then slowly, beautifully, they darkened. As the biscuits flattened, I swelled. As the surfaces cracked like the picture in the recipe I burst with pride.

Twenty-five minutes later I drew from the oven seventeen perfect gingernuts. I laid them on the wire cooling tray known as the kitchen bench, and dashed to the phone to boast to the woman who knows. She was out.

Having hauled the dogs off the bench I cooled the eleven gingernuts by blowing on them. Then I picked one up. It was as hard as an ice-hockey puck, a tooth buster, the real thing. I made a coffee. I dunked the biscuit. It disintegrated. I did a little jig. After forty-one years I had filled my tins.

Twenty Yak

There comes a moment in the life of any smoker when he knows with sudden certainty that he will never smoke another cigarette. This moment normally occurs in hospital and is followed by a dramatic fall in body temperature.

When I enter Mastermind, smoking will be my specialist topic. I took up smoking at just the right age and did not, as so many of my contemporaries did, give up when we moved on to secondary school. I also smoked for all the right reasons; viz. sex, sport and poverty. Anyone who knows me now will confirm my prowess in just over 30% of these. In other words, then, I reckon I know a thing or two about smoking.

That, however, was until today. For today I rang the editor of *The Press*. I'll rephrase that. Today I rang THE EDITOR OF *THE PRESS*, an august gentleman, immune to capital-letter flattery and sporting one of those Frank Nobilo beards of stubble which I've never quite understood. What I don't understand is how they tend them. Is there some sort of shaver like a ride-on mower that is sold only to golfers and prominent, stately editors who are no doubt also nifty with the five-iron?

Anyway THE EDITOR OF *THE PRESS* and I got chatting, as one does with editors, about cigarettes, and HE said some frightfully kind things about my rate of consumption. Was HE a smoker, I asked. It turned out that THE EDITOR OF *THE PRESS* was an ex-smoker, which I've always thought, as I told HIM, to be the very best type of smoker. How, I asked, did he stop? And HE said, 'Yak.'

See what a pithy man HE is. Yak. It's a beautiful answer. Economical, trenchant, enigmatic, editory. I was impressed. THE EDITOR OF *THE PRESS* didn't get where HE is today by beating about the bush. Ask HIM a straight question and HE'LL say, 'Yak.'

It transpired that Yak is a brand of Nepalese cigarette popular with the more suicidal Sherpas. A few beards ago THE EDITOR OF THE PRESS was in Nepal – well-travelled too, you see – and faced with a cash-flow crisis. American cigarettes were beyond his pocket and Yak, though less than a dong for a packet of twenty, were, as HE put it, 'guaranteed tonsilitis'. So HE gave up. Just like that. There's character. There's strength. There's what this country needs a bit more of. And that's exactly what I told HIM, in a most unobsequious man-to-man way.

But for those of us who flounder a little lower on the evolutionary ladder than editors, stopping smoking is less straightforward. I've had a dab or two at it myself. I could never get a decent drag out of those patch things, and the chewing gum stuff was so bitter that I had to have a coffee to take the taste away, and as even the simplest chemist knows, coffee grounds + H_2O (heated) = unquenchable lust for a cigarette.

Of course, one can go the organic route. I have in front of me the 'Wise Woman's Tips for Giving up Smoking.' They include, 'Bring home a flower', 'Eat a wild salad – even if it's only one dandelion leaf', and, top of the list, 'Take an oat-straw bath.' All great fun as I am sure you agree, but in my 'garden' it's hard to know if you've got to the dandelion before the dogs have, so I just brought a flower home and ate it. This necessitated a coffee to take the taste away.

Sprawled in my oat-straw bath with *The Press* and twenty Rothmans I saw an ad in the personal column. 'Stop smoking the easy way... Hypnosis.'

Now, I owe a lot to my mother. She taught me how to know when a sponge is cooked, which strangers to accept lifts from (the wealthy ones), and a method of gripping the carotid artery that I have never seen bettered. (On the famous night when she caught the burglar *in flagrante* and the spare bedroom, the police had to ring around for his dental records.)

What my mother never told me, however, and finding it out for myself has cost me time, money and tears, was to shun all people with framed diplomas on the wall.

The hypnotist's wall was more diplomas than wall. Pride of place went to an ornate little number reading, 'The Bulawayo Centre for Hypnosis, Naturopathy and Proctoscopy. Weekend residential course. Pass with distinction.' It had a big red seal.

I paid $70 to the hypnotist, who was wearing a golf-club sweater but didn't have a proper beard, and then I conned him. I did this by pretending to be hypnotised when I wasn't. I closed my eyes and breathed slowly and spoke robotically. He was completely taken in.

The moment it was over I went straight round to the dairy for twenty Yak. They were out of Yak, so I had to settle for Camel on the grounds of their similar exotic shagginess, and then I lounged against a lamp-post opposite the hypnotist's diploma-laden house and smoked ostentatiously. It was one of those moments of triumph, rather like talking man-to-man and straight up with THE EDITOR OF THE PRESS. Such things make life worth living.

Plane greetings

There was a toddler at the airport. The toddler seemed to have two mothers. Neither of them seemed to like him much. The toddler was entertaining those of us who were waiting in the terminal by ramming us with a luggage trolley. When one or other of his mothers told him off he entertained us further by wailing.

I had come to greet friends from Canada. Travelling is harrowing, and after a long flight people should not have to deal alone with the rigours of a foreign airport. I like to give them a warm, human, southern welcome and offer to help them carry their duty-free goods.

I had also come to inspect the new international terminal since my invitation to the gala opening went astray in the post. I am pleased to report that the new terminal has every appearance of an airport terminal. The architects, Messrs Bland, Synthetic and Pastel, have built a terminal which would merge indistinguishably into any airport in the world.

Travel is traumatic. It wrenches us from the familiar, strips us of the homes and possessions that identify us. You can see on the faces of travellers that they are vulnerable, like hermit crabs scuttling between shells. Perhaps it is to soothe the traveller that all airports are built of the same materials which I cannot name but which owe nothing to nature. Technology whisks the traveller round the globe and squirts him out into the same air-conditioning, automatic plate-glass doors, wiry carpet and recessed lighting that he left in Los Angeles or London, Bangkok or Budapest.

When passengers finally emerge through the doors that say 'Welcome to Christchurch' they find themselves in an identity parade. Several hundred pairs of eyes look up to take them in. It's a hostile welcome.

Every international flight carries the same human freight. The pilots appear first, striding manfully with their natty overnight bags, their uniforms, and their deep smug tans. Then come the stewardesses, their professional manner relaxed a little but still decked out like dolls in national dress. After them the passengers.

The young travel like snails with gargantuan backpacks. If they fall over they can't get up. They do not expect to be greeted. They travel not to enjoy but to endure. They stagger through the terminal and seek out the backpackers' minibus with its hard cheap seats.

Returning tourists are boisterous. They sport unfortunate shirts, Hawaiian hats and suntans that have happened too suddenly.

Middle-aged couples are not boisterous. The husband pushes the trolley of luggage and the wife steadies it with a single hand, perhaps to retain contact with her identity, or to ward off thieves in a strange land or to ensure that her man doesn't bolt. He doesn't look like bolting.

Few people greet well. Our lives are placid and we are ill-suited to the drama of separation or reunion. The high-voltage of emotion discomforts us. Some lovers wrap round each other like vines, but most plant awkward inaccurate kisses and then look at their shoes. Men greet men with a clumsy one-armed embrace which doubles as a backslap.

And when the greetings are over, everyone talks about what the weather has been like.

The toddler, I discovered, did not have two mothers. He had three. The third was his real mum who had been to Sydney. When she appeared through the glass doors her eyes found her baby instantly. She abandoned her trolley and ran to her little piece of flesh. The little piece ran towards her, then stopped and ducked behind a chair. He pouted. He was telling her off for deserting him.

She knelt and spread her arms wide. She was crying. The little monster held off for a few cruel seconds then the pull grew too strong and he hurtled into her arms as if by suction and exploded into tears. His legs wrapped around her ribs like a chimp's legs. His arms circled her neck and he sank his face into her hair. Mother and son fitted together like pieces of a jigsaw puzzle. And they stayed where they were, entwined and rocking, a Henry Moore statue made flesh, oblivious to the world. Soldiers could not have separated them.

I heard mother promise her child that she would never ever go away again, and then, like his two other mothers and everyone else, I had to turn away because in the midst of the sterile airport terminal I found my eyes were pricking.

At that point my Canadian friends arrived and were so moved by my obvious emotion at seeing them that they gave me a bottle of scotch and 200 cigarettes and simply refused to hear of payment.

At the Sign of
the Stabbed Dog

Even little men dream. Five foot three in my stockinged feet, five eight on Saturday evenings in my Chanel stilettos, I had a dream.

That I was able to live that dream, I owe to my Uncle Larry. When Uncle Larry popped his cork in the mid-eighties and his mid-fifties after a long and prosperous career as a pioneer of massage in Waimate I discovered I was the sole relation who had not disowned him. He left me a wad of Brierley shares and a mountain of used lingerie. I knew immediately what I had to do.

Retaining only the slinkiest of the lingerie for recreational purposes, I bulldozed the rest into a brown paper parcel the size of Fendalton and posted it to Fendalton where it won several architectural awards in which I took no interest for I had other plans. I was going to buy a bookshop.

I had my eye on a dank little establishment off Manchester Street. It came with a somnolent labrador, a skeletal staff and the complete 1871 quarto edition of Browning's poetical works in pink calfskin uncut. Thither on an unforgettable hot January afternoon in '86 I flounced, pushed open the door and sank a four inch sequinned stiletto into the snoozing labrador. It flicked open an eyelid.

The burly proprietor of dog and shop rose to protest but from my clutch bag I drew the Brierley wad, peeled off three non-debentured scrips and waved them under his nose. The intoxicating fragrance of wealth wafted up each of those heavy hair-lined nostrils and turned his head. With a deft tweak of the nose hair I twisted it back to face me, and talked turkey. His years in Constantinople had served him well, and within five minutes he had skipped out of the door and off to Manchester Street with his Brierleys waving in the breeze. The shop was mine – lock, stock, barrel, dog, uncut Browning and skeletal staff.

I knew what I had to do and I did it. The Canterbury Museum expressed delight at my offer of the skeletal staff so I lugged the three of them out to the Morris Oxford and rattled off down Worcester Boulevard in those pre-boulevard days when Worcester was merely saucy. A traffic officer hauled me over. He was a muscular man and there seemed little point in hauling back. He accused me of running a red light, but as I explained to him, he had mistaken me for my old Uncle Larry. The officer changed the charge to speeding. I was bound for the hospital, I told him, and indicated the skeletal staff nodding behind me. It was, I said, something of an emergency. He blanched agreeably and waved me on.

Back at the shop I tossed the lock, stock and a Collected Ursula Bethell into the barrel which I then rolled into the oblivion of the backyard. Mine would be no antiquarian bookshop. I intended to be at the cutting edge of contemporary literature, giving the book-buying public of New Zealand what it didn't yet know it wanted.

With my unerring eye for a sales gimmick I left the stiletto in the labrador – besides, the dog had taken to chewing at the sequins with every appearance of affection. We opened in May. Sporting an elaborate corsage of darling buds much shaken by the rough winds, I cut the ribbon that barred the doors of 'The Stabbed Dog' and invited the hordes to flock.

Initially we specialised in self-improvement and we rapidly got better. *How to Make Your First Million Without Raising a Finger* sold solidly. Within two weeks every manicurist in town had a copy. *Your Route to Fendalton* found favour with lost souls, but it wasn't until we hit the rugby market that we really began to shovel the spondulicks.

Those old and elegant stalwarts, *Game for a Ruck*, *An Illustrated History of Rucking*, and *Ruck Me Tender* soon had the tills ringing a merry tune which drew patrons from the pavement just to listen. And we found our first runaway bestseller in Olo Brown's autobiography with its ground-breaking scratch'n'sniff chapter on liniments.

As we lounged in Le Bon Bolli one decadent lunchtime over a platter of hogs' trotters the dog suggested that without rugby we'd be an illiterate nation. I scoffed of course but when he told me he had sold the Ursula Bethell that morning on the pretext that she'd been physiotherapist for the 1921 Invincibles I had to eat my words. They sat uncomfortably with the trotters until lubricated with a goblet of the blushful Bledisloe, its oval bubbles winking at the brim.

The late eighties were heady days as we expanded exponentially, so exponentially indeed that we had to forgo Le Bon Bolli and snack on diet books. All the while we extended our repertoire. We followed up the smash hit *Kiwi Men and Their Sheds* with *Kiwi Women and Their Garages, Kiwi Children and Their Orphanages* and *Kiwi Kiwis and Their Burrows*. Copies of *Men are Forwards; Women are Backs* found their way onto every single woman's bedside table and we had to employ an army of private dicks to fetch them back which proved a popular move.

Eventually we divided the shop into five sections: rugby; self-improvement; romance; kiwiana; and books based on BBC television programmes. The rest, as you know, is history.

Initially the history sold poorly but then the labrador came up with the idea of screwing chair legs into the corners of the James Beliches and created single-pawed the market for coffee-table books.

It is not given to everyone to fulfil a dream. It was given to me. I am proud of what I did. Having established the formula for every major book retailer in the country I sold *The Stabbed Dog* to a Brierley's consortium in 1991 and went to live happily ever after in Waimate with the lingerie, the Browning and the labrador.

A thumb in the air

My favourite short story is called 'Annie' by Jim Crace. The narrator is hitching from solitude in Nevada to his wife in New York and gets a lift in a stolen car. The car's called Annie. The driver's a crim on the run. Neither driver nor narrator has money for gas, so they pick up hitch-hikers who chip in a few dollars. When the driver suspects that one of the hitch-hikers has rumbled him, he runs away in the night and they drive on without him. The cast of hitch-hikers in the car keeps changing. When the narrator reaches New York he leaves Annie to its occupants. Years later he sees Annie again in Louisiana. It's still full of people.

I thought of the story today because I picked up a hitch-hiker. She was seventeen, pretty and she wore jeans in the way that only seventeen-year-old girls can wear jeans. That helped of course, but had she been seventeen stone and armed I would have picked her up because I have taken a vow.

For ten years of my life I hitched everywhere. What prompted me to hitch was that most primitive, simple and honourable of human urges, poverty. It wasn't until I was twenty-eight that I bought my first car, the Whale. It cost me six pints of Bass and a prawn curry. On the day I acquired it, I vowed I would not drive past a hitch-hiker and I have kept my vow except for people with beards, be they men or women.

The girl wanted to go to New Brighton.

'Hop in,' I said. She scanned the two large and slavering dogs in the back seat. She scanned the empty passenger seat beside me. She got in the back. The dogs were thrilled.

She spoke little. All I could get out of her was that she worked in a pizza parlour. Her silence may have stemmed from the dogs trying to lick her into submission, but that silence reminded me of an unsavoury lad I went to school with, called Pete Thrale.

When we left school, Pete and I went our separate ways: I to university, Pete to any place he could rob. But five years later we met on a motorway intersection near Cricklewood. Pete was waving a huge cardboard arm with the legend 'Entertaining Hitch-hikers Ltd'. We got a lift within minutes, whereupon Pete folded his cardboard arm, stuffed it in his rucksack, climbed into the back seat of the car and went to sleep. It was left to me to make conversation with the driver, a sales rep for Marmite, as far as Leeds where he was attending a conference called Spreading the Spreads.

Pete was heading on to Scotland, but we stayed an hour in Leeds, had a beer together, rediscovered our mutual dislike, then went our separate ways once more, this time for ever. But before we did, Pete gave me a jar of Marmite. He hated the stuff, he said.

Hitching's like that. It's random, shapeless, thrilling and boring in turns. No two journeys are the same. It's also the nearest thing there is to practical socialism. Nevertheless it's a very good thing. The poor get a free ride; the rich get company. Everyone wins.

People will tell you that hitch-hiking is dangerous. It is. People die hitch-hiking. But they also die on the lavatory, in front of the television or *in flagrante delicto*.

The danger of hitch-hiking is that crazy people pick you up. The glory of hitch-hiking, on the other hand, is that crazy people pick you up. I remember a Frenchman with a battered Citroen and a face like an aubergine.

I said I wanted to go to Angoulême.

'Oh really,' he said, 'my mother's in hospital in Angoulême. Get in.'

I said I was sorry about his mother and we discussed her condition. I tried him on other topics but none interested him. When I ran out of mother questions we fell silent.

At a turn-off to Bordeaux, which lay 200k to the south-west, a boy and a girl were hitching. Monsieur Aubergine stopped. The boy and the girl said they wanted to go to Bordeaux.

'Oh really,' said Monsieur Aubergine, 'my mother's in hospital in Bordeaux. Get in.'

Then he told me to get out because I was boring. I walked through midday heat into Angoulême and found a man asleep on a park bench with a lead draped loosely on his arm. At the business end of the lead, and also asleep, lay an adult male lion. As I have said, hitching's like that. By nature I am neither brave nor adventurous, but hitching thrust adventures on me. No other activity has given me such stories, such horror, such wonder, such fear, such raw and random life.

I drive little these days, but I seem to see fewer hitch-hikers on the road every year. Perhaps the young have cars now, perhaps the safety sermons have got to them, I don't know, but the girl from Brighton was the first hitch-hiker I have picked up for six months. When we stopped by the pier and she peeled the dogs off, thanked me and walked for ever into somewhere else, I was stabbed by nostalgia and by envy.

Wise fools

I have got into the habit of getting older, and the older I get the more I relish the oxymoron.

I came to the oxymoron late in life and at first I struggled to believe that such a luscious word existed. But exist it does, deriving from the Greek oxys, meaning sharp, and moros, foolish. Thus it means something pointedly foolish, an apparent contradiction, the sort of thing a fool might say which makes no literal sense but which approaches the truth more nearly than something a wise man might say. Hurry slowly is an example.

Shakespeare knew all about oxymorons. He had Juliet tell Romeo that parting is such sweet sorrow and we haven't stopped saying it since. Shakepeare's fools are among his wisest characters. The fool in King Lear sees through every other character in the play. The fool is weak and strong, funny and sad, loving and bitter. He's an oxymoron in motley.

Conversely many of Shakespeare's wise men are fools; Polonius tells us

> This above all: to thine own self be true,
> And it must follow, as the night the day,
> Thou canst not then be false to any man.

High counsel from the lips of a dingbat, a man stuffed with vanity, pompous as a dowager and scheming as a rat. When Polonius finally collects a sword through the arras and gurgles his life away we rejoice every bit as much as we grieve.

Cue for another oxymoron, schadenfreude, a typically tuneful term from that Lego language German, meaning joy at another's distress. How we would like to deny schadenfreude but the ratings tell the real story. For what is it that over a third of the population seeks when it turns on the television at six o'clock each evening if it is not the thrill of other people's suffering? It is not information; you will find better information in the pub. Indeed, the very phrase 'television news' is an oxymoron.

No, we watch the news to see the mother of three weep at their funeral. We watch it to see the relatives of kidnap victims turn the mournful pages of the photograph album and, if we are lucky, collapse before the camera's Cyclopean, dispassionate eye. We watch it to see the missiles fired from the USS Wallopem in the Adriatic and we want to see them land. Though we may con ourselves with a moral stance, with the tut-tuts of sympathy, side by side on the sofa with our better nature sits Sister Schadenfreude, whispering that we are oxymorons too.

Oxymorons are easy to invent – I think immediately of National Party think-tank, or committee decision, or Black Cap victory or the Australian Journal of Philosophy – but there is no need to invent oxymorons, for they surround us at every instant of our lives. Fun run is an oxymoron. Parliamentary debate is an oxymoron. President Clinton is an oxymoron. Health service, keeping a secret, moderate drinking, true love, Grey Power, ninety-nine per cent fat free, modern art, Pacific Ocean, Happy Christmas – the list is endless.

Alexander Pope, the eighteenth-century poet, best summarises why that list is endless. Pope was stunted and malformed – he couldn't stand erect without a heavy-duty corset – and yet he towered above his contemporaries. He was peevish and venomous and yet he attained a sweetness of voice and a clarity of mind that few can rival.

Himself an oxymoron, Pope wrote of mankind in oxymoronic terms. He called man 'a being darkly wise and rudely great.' He said we were 'born but to die, and reasoning but to err,' that we were,

> Created half to rise, and half to fall;
> Great Lord of all things, yet a prey to all;
> Sole judge of truth, in endless error hurled:
> The glory, jest and riddle of the world!

And so it is, in this mad and lovely life, that the oxymoron, which makes no sense, makes sense.

Just visiting

A needle sticks out of the back of my hand. From the needle a pipe snakes up to a plastic bag hung on a sort of hatstand. A valve shows saline solution and penicillin dripping out of the bag and into my vein.

The last night I spent in hospital was the first night of my life. I do not recall it clearly. I recall last night, however, with great clarity, how at 2.30am I assumed the foetal position, went in for some serious whimpering, and admitted myself to this huge building. Something had happened to my throat which prevented speech, hampered breathing, and brought pain, panic and a quantity of clear, gelatinous mucus which would have invited juicy metaphors had I been in metaphoric mood. With my windpipe closing I was not in metaphoric mood.

In the emergency ward they laid me down and hooked me to a sci-fi machine which probed my ear and gripped my arm and finger and produced a screenful of information about how I was. Not who or what I was, but how. It told my temperature, the pressure and oxygen loading of my blood and the seismographic read-out of my pulse, reminiscent of scenes in bad American soap operas when Mary-Lou's eyelids flutter and the camera turns to the screen where the read-out falters and flattens into a line and Mary-Lou meets her maker. I think of Mary-Lou now. I did not think of her at 2.30 this morning. Then, stupefied, I stared at a spot on the wall and urged them silently to take the pain away. They did. I loved them.

Freed from pain I was able to look around the emergency ward, to take in the vital signs about vital signs, a warning notice about Viagra, the spectacular pieces of machinery, the open cupboard of bandages, drugs and, inexplicably, a huge bottle of DYC malt vinegar. Then they drugged me and wheeled me into a corner to sleep. I woke in the morning to find myself tagged like a dog and dressed in a smock. I wanted to leave but they wheeled me to see the man who knows about ears, noses and throats.

Being wheeled in a smock clutching a brown paper bag holding the clothes I had arrived in, confirmed that I was sick and different. I sat below the eye level of the healthy. We wheeled along swabbed lino, past walls of hospital green, deeper and deeper into the building, passing old people who seemed to live there, bent, gnarled, thin of hair and frail of bone, resigned to the indignities of suffering. Through lifts and corridors we travelled further and further from the exit.

The specialist dropped a snake down my nose, a snake with a light on its tip to illuminate my pharynx, larynx and points south. Three ridiculously young medical students took turns to peer into me. 'That's the voice box,' said the specialist as a girl with a ponytail bent over the snake. 'Say aaah.' I said aaah. 'Cool,' said the girl, and then, 'Thank you.'

While waiting for a bed I sat in a day room with a pile of last year's *Woman's Weeklies*, a book called *Born Again* by one of Nixon's Watergate cronies who got God, and a large-print text called *Death of an Author*. I tried *Born Again*. It stank. In the corner, the television played *5.30 with Jude* at 9.30 in the morning and no one seemed to mind. Time makes no sense in hospital. The place runs on slow biological time. It is always running out.

Television land is fantasy land, the land at the end of the rainbow. More poignant is the view from the window. Beyond the glass lies the mundane world, the park, the streets, the people going to work, the land I come from and to which I long to return. I shall. Some in here won't.

All the nurses on my ward are women, kind, skilled and underpaid. A few address their patients as if they are deaf cretins, but most simply care and take pleasure from caring. But I do not want to be nursed. I resist them. Hospital reduces you to two things – your vital signs and a childish state where mummy does things for you. I am too vain to release that sense of my own invulnerability and independence. I do not belong in mortality house. Not yet.

An hour ago a nurse brought me a magazine. Inside lay a box of matches and a single cigarette. I could have kissed her. She pretended to be ashamed of what she had done, but was clearly pleased to please. Feeling like a fugitive I headed down the corridor to the lift, towing my hatstand. It had spastic wheels, like a super-market trolley. I found it easier to carry it. Down five floors I went, then out through automatic doors to Hagley Park and the edge of reality. Ducks, gulls and sky. Still dressed in a smock and um-bilically linked to my drip I lit my cigarette.

'You're Joe Barnett, aren't you?' said a woman in a coat.

I admitted it.

'What are you doing here?' she asked.

'Just visiting,' I said. And I meant it.